PRAISE FOR HONEST RICHES

"I would not be where I am today if it wasn't for this brilliant young lady. I am blown away by her altruism. Holly gives total commitment to helping others. Now I do Internet Online Marketing and make more money than when I was a Corporate Computer Systems Engineer working for an extremely large International Company."

– CRAIG PERI, Entrepreneur Lifestyles

"This program is without a doubt the most informative and accurate program I've come across. Her program has something for everyone and WILL make you money if you follow her lead. Her support is exceptional and she has a genuine desire to help those in her program succeed. Highly recommended!"

– TOBY, HonestAudits.com

"I highly recommend Holly's book to anyone that I come across online, as it was where I got my start. She has personally helped me to change the path and the success in my life. Holly's book Honest Riches has become one of the internet's top selling books for learning how to market online."

–DAVIN OGDEN

"I bought Holly's book nine months ago, there was great information in it and the online support was out of this world. I'm now paying off my mortgage thanks to Holly."

– MARK LITTLEWOOD

"[Honest Riches] is virtually a pre-requisite read if you plan on learning & earning from the wonderful world of internet marketing. I can honestly say that Honest Riches is the only e-book you ever really need to buy if you want to get the 'how-to' on internet marketing. Once I put some strategies into action, I made my very first sale & have continued to do so."

– NAHLIA WILLEMS, Net Marketing for Newbies

HONEST RICHES

Comprehensive Guide
to Making Money Online

✦

Holly Mann

The Honest Riches book is also available in electronic format. The book is available online at: http://www.HonestHolly.com.

ISBN: 978-0-578-00195-1

This book is dedicated to God.

"For I know the plans I have for you,
plans to prosper you and not to harm
you, plans to give you hope and a future."
-Jeremiah 29:11

TABLE OF CONTENTS

FOREWORD

Holly Mann is one of the most influential online marketers of our time. From her humble beginnings Holly has taken a simple vision of being self supportive, and has turned it into a movement online that is surely not to be repeated anytime soon. Her compassion for helping people to succeed online, and in life, is being gently passed on from one person to the next and is changing the face of internet marketing as we know it.

Holly's approach with her marketing and with her life has always been centered on complete honesty with herself and for those she comes into contact with. The positive experience that people have felt by her presence in their lives has in one form or another resulted in an energy that has affected the lives of thousands.

She has a very rare gift of touching people in a way which helps remind them that there is hope and beauty remaining in this world, and it all begins with each one of us.

It's in this gift that she has passes on, that has created people involved with doing business online in changing their values, their integrity and their honesty with not only themselves but to each other. The people being influenced are helping one another to become successful more than ever before.

The first time I'd ever spoken or shared any words with Holly was back in late 2006 as a result of meeting her in the Honest Work from Home Success forum she'd created. It's extremely hard to explain, but, just from those first few simple transactions of communication with her, I could tell that there was something very special about this young woman.

Today, there isn't one shred of a doubt in my mind, that Holly Mann was placed in my life for a reason. I could feel the kind and positive spirit that was emulating from inside this girl even though she was thousands of miles away. It's as if God had placed her there on that day for the specific purpose of letting me know that I was making the proper decision with my life. It was a feeling that I don't think I will ever find words, but, will never forget for as long as I live.

If you would have told me back at that time prior to meeting Holly that I was going to be witnessing some of the most amazing and inspiring events I'd ever seen in my life, I'm sure I would have been hard pressed to believe it.

We were watching people from all reaches of the planet bond in helping each other to overcome the obstacles they faced. Her forum became a place that didn't know anything about nationality, sex, religion, color, or anything else that unfortunately sometimes separates people in this world.

This was true human compassion and caring amongst people, giving and helping one another in the pursuit of a happier life. There was a lot more going on with it than just internet marketing. It had to do with people helping to save each other's lives. It has been and continues to be an experience I'm sure all of us involved hold very close to our hearts.

The methods that Holly teaches in her book are not based on theory as you will find in many e-books out there. The teachings that Holly passes on, are based entirely on the methods that have been proven to work for her time and time again. If something didn't work, you won't find it in the book. She only knows how to pass on real concrete methods of working online that are known to generate income if you follow the methods set forth. She takes the guess work of trial and error out of the equation, since they are the exact methods that she has used to create a very good sustainable income. There is no doubt, that if you work diligently, consistently, and continuously towards achieving your goals, it is inevitable that you will have success. I've come to know Holly as a close friend now, and I know firsthand that she wishes you success in every aspect of your life.

Please use the information that Holly lays out for you, and continue in her quest to revolutionize online marketing by passing on the same values that she has instilled in so many of us. If we can all continue to treat one another with respect, honesty, and genuinely care about one another in this world, it will continue to grow and will have an impacting effect on the new and upcoming generation of students in this business. Holly Mann's purpose in this world is clear. She brings to the world hope, joy, and true conviction of values among fellow human beings. It's bringing people together and helping them to believe in themselves and their dreams once again. Holly is a special gift of love to this great planet we have. The people that have been blessed to come to know her completely cherish the beautiful generous spirit that she is. Thank you Holly, and don't ever stop believing.

Davin Ogden, "The Davinator"
CEO Groovytastic Empire
http://honestholly.com/goto/davin

ABOUT THE AUTHOR

My name is Holly Beth Mann, and I first started working online when I was 21-years-old. When I began, I had no experience or knowledge of Internet Marketing. I also had very little money to spare, so I spent all of my free time learning (by observing how other Internet Marketers created their success). I evaluated their strategies and it began to make sense to me. When I began my endeavor online, I was a single mother with a 4 month old son. I could hardly make ends meet. Prior, I worked as a journalist in the Army and then as a civil contractor in Iraq – always struggling to save money.

I was living with family in the United States when my son was 4 months old. I decided to take a leap of faith and do something drastic. I told family members that we would be moving to Thailand (where I had lived previously as an exchange student in high school).

Then, I sold everything that we owned, and purchased two one-way airline tickets to Thailand. I knew that I could afford to live there, while getting my internet business off the ground.

I am a stubborn person and did not want to burden others by living with them. I also didn't want to leave my baby in a day care facility, so I could go off and work a normal job. I felt this was my opportunity to make a change.

My son and I survived the long 22 hour flight across the globe and we finally settled in. Thailand brought with it struggle after struggle, but we pushed forth. After arriving in Thailand, I could not afford a new computer. I sold my laptop to pay for part of our airline tickets to Thailand. For approximately $250 USD, I purchased all of the used computer parts needed to "create" a working computer. The person, who sold it to me, also put it together at no extra cost.

The computer was unsightly; it was loud and made a buzzing sound after it was on for an hour or so. I feared it would stop working at any time. But the computer survived, as did I. Through my sheer desperation to make a positive change for my son and our futures, I kept learning all that I could take in. I slept very little for the first four months, but it paid off (literally). By the fourth month of this tireless relentless learning and applying, I made my first $12,000 USD. That is how it all began. It was a huge triumph for me to see such a severe increase in my income – and to have it grow over the years. Life became brighter and eventually my son and I expanded our horizons. We travelled and lived in Malta for several months (an island off of the Mediterranean, south of Sicily). We upgraded our living arrangements and moved into a condominium in northern Thailand. Eventually we moved back to the U.S.A. I feel grateful for this journey and path my life has taken, and most grateful to be in a position that I can help others as well.

I feel honored to share my story with you, and to share all of the steps to my success. I want you to achieve your goals and live your dreams. No longer just survive, but thrive in what you do every single day. If you are living your life in a constant battle to pay the bills and just make it by – this guide is for you.

I've created Honest Riches to provide you with the most profitable, up-to-date, useful ways to create income stream(s) online in the least amount of time, through a range of methods. My approach in teaching you the techniques is one that is honest and real. I try to be transparent with my life and with the guide. With Honest Riches, my goal is to give you all the tools to achieve ultimate financial success with the methods outlined.

I have used and continually use every method that is described in this guide, so you have every resource to prosper. The methods work. If you have the will-power, you can open the doors to your financial freedom. Years ago I knew nothing of what is described in the following pages. Continuously learning and staying up-to-date with the trends and ever-changing technologies can be an exhaustive task. The purpose of this guide is to provide you a much less-arduous path to creating wealth online. I sincerely hope that the knowledge gained from reading the guide will change your income, your life and allow you the financial security that you are striving for. This book will give you all the tools; you just need to be ready to dig into it.

To Your Success...
Holly Beth Mann
http://www.HonestHolly.com

ABOUT THE BOOK

Honest Riches is a comprehensive internet marketing guide, providing you with the tools to succeed in the ever-changing highly profitable field. The purpose is to allow you to create multiple income streams from the comfort of your home. Internet Marketing comprises of online advertising methods, search engine optimization, e-mail marketing, research and niche-development, website creation and Affiliate Marketing & promotional methods.

Honest Riches will teach you how to conduct research to know what's popular and what is not, both online and in the public sector. You will be aware of what keywords and key phrases people are typing in Google and other search engines daily, how to find niches, how to promote a product with or without a website, Search Engine Optimization (SEO) and how to bring all of the methods together. Affiliate Marketing is extremely profitable because when applied in correlation with my other techniques, you can create an income (or several income streams), which will require no selling, no inventory and no customer support (unless you create and sell your own product).

If the Internet Marketing terms used in the above paragraphs sound like a foreign language to you – do not be alarmed. Definitions of terms can be found throughout the book.

There is also an index, so you can lookup specific words and find their page numbers and locations throughout the guide. If still unsure, it might help to do some independent research online.

For those readers with little or no experience working online, you do not need to know how to be a web designer or have any other lavish computer-related skills to be successful with the techniques. It's important to have an open-mind, a willingness to learn and expand your knowledge, be focused and driven to succeed.

People learn at different rates and through different means, so throughout the book I offer a variety of techniques to suit a range of preferences. Although most of the techniques are free, I also offer additional ways to achieve results, which may require a small investment. It's important that I cover all options in order to guide all of the different readers. Some people have less time and don't mind spending a few dollars to pay someone to complete their task, as others prefer to do everything on their own.

How the Book is Structured

Honest Riches is divided into 10 books, which all contain related chapters and sections. You are not required to read it in order, but I do recommend that you at least look it all over before beginning a new project that utilizes the techniques. The reason being, you may end up reading something in a later chapter that would be more suitable and useful for the project you are creating.

Please note that all of the hyperlinks in the book are cloaked. This is because when links change or are no longer available, rather than re-creating an entire book and sending it out to the masses, I can change the cloaked link through my website (and the link will be repaired without editing your book). This way, you will always be up-to-date with the correct information and resources.

So, all of the links will start out with http://www.honestholly.com/goto/ and end with this: ...I want to reassure you before you begin reading, that I will only mention and vouch for a program if I 100% fully stand by it.

My Vision

My vision is to provide you with the most accurate, up-to-date useful and profitable Internet Marketing techniques. I will continually learn, apply and personally try everything I can, so I can keep you informed. That way, you save your valuable time by avoiding the useless or fruitless endeavors.

Book 1

Affiliate Marketing

CHAPTER 1: AFFILIATE MARKETING BASICS

Affiliate Marketing Defined

Affiliate Marketing is a lucrative, high-paying venture to break into. You can be your own boss, make your own hours, have your own business, yet have no inventory or major overhead costs to be concerned with. It is extremely risky for the average person interested in becoming a business owner through creating, manufacturing, patenting and selling their own product.

Few small-businesses push through and succeed past their first year. For the rest of us, let's assume, you do not have your own product to sell but would like to enjoy the independence of making your own hours, working online as you please and having full financial stability.

Affiliate Marketing offers the benefits of having your own business and products without having to deal with the risks involved. It encompasses tactics used to gain exposure for a company online through allowing Internet Marketers to promote company products and earn commissions on sales. Most businesses online have what is called an affiliate program. Affiliate programs are free to join and allow you the ability to promote that company's product or service and earn an income through doing so.

How It Works

The following scenario is an example of how a person might profit with affiliate marketing. Pretend you have just created your first website. You have an interest in one particular internet marketing guru. You've done your research and you know that people are looking for information about him online. Your first website is all about him; his past, his biography, and schooling and about his products.

You've signed up with his affiliate program (by going to his official website and looking for an "Affiliates" link, then joining). On your website you write about his products, and next to each small summary you have used your affiliate link that says "Click Here to Learn More about It" – which will drive those visitors to his sales page and official website. A percentage of the visitors that your site receives will end up buying something from the official website. Those visitors who have specifically clicked through your affiliate link (with or without knowing it) and purchased, will earn you a large 50% commission on all resulting sales. Plain and simple – that is how it works (commissions vary according to the program). The key to that scenario working successfully is for your website to gain a high ranking for specific keywords or key phrases related to that popular internet marketing guru. The process of having your website reach a high ranking online for certain keywords is called Search Engine Optimization (SEO). You will learn all about Search Engine Optimization (SEO) in Book 5.

Joining Affiliate Programs

Once you sign up to join an affiliate program, you will be given a unique ID and a unique affiliate link that you can use to drive traffic to that company's website. The person promoting the products is the affiliate and the company with the products is the merchant. You can promote that company through online forums, through e-mails or on a website.

Although most affiliate programs are free to join, some do require that you purchase the product before promoting it as an affiliate. It's a logical prerequisite because you should know the product prior to advocating it to others. When interested readers click through your unique affiliate link and decide to make a purchase from the merchant, then you will be given a percentage of the profits or certain amount of money per-sale or per-lead.

Affiliate programs use advanced tracking techniques and cookies to ensure that the affiliate is paid for their efforts. Affiliate Marketing is my key to financial success online. But it does not stand-alone. Making money online month after month requires more than just knowledge of how to place a link on a website or in a forum.

Anyone can sign up to become an affiliate, but a true affiliate marketer must equip himself/herself with the tools, resources and techniques to create an automated, profitable income stream. Honest Riches provides you with all of the methods needed to do so. Businesses create affiliate programs because it helps drive targeted traffic to their website without having to pay for extremely high advertising costs.

The business owner's website will then receive traffic which it may not otherwise have had. Now that you understand the basic concept of affiliate marketing, we can take the explanation a bit further. The following chapter will describe what affiliate networks are for, and how you can benefit from joining them.

CHAPTER 2: AFFILIATE NETWORKS

Affiliate Network Basics

When business owners decide to create an affiliate program for their product or service, they can choose to do so through a variety of methods. Software programs can be purchased online; uploaded and installed so that the company has their own affiliate program setup.

The person's company would personally manage their affiliate program and they would be responsible for sending out checks or payments to the affiliates promoting for them. That type of affiliate program could be classified as an independent affiliate program.

Independent affiliate programs generally require the person or business to have a website hosted and online. For business owners who do not want to deal with the tracking, payments and the workload involved with having an independent affiliate program, they may choose to sign-up with an affiliate network. Affiliate networks do the work for the businesses and manage an array of affiliate programs in one place. For people who work online and promote multiple products through different websites, it can be difficult to keep track of all of them.

Affiliate networks differ because once you sign-up to be a part of the affiliate network, then you generally have access to promoting a large variety of products for different merchants or companies. You may login to the affiliate network and then browse different affiliate programs based on criteria such as: Health and Fitness, Home and Family, Internet, Money and Employment. You can also usually search for an affiliate program based on a keyword or search term/phrase.

With an affiliate network, all of your earnings are managed through your account control panel and payments are consolidated so that you receive your check or direct deposit with all profits at once (rather than multiple checks from different companies).

Basically, affiliate networks are comprised of a lot of affiliate programs. It makes it easy for merchants and prospective affiliates to "meet" and create partnerships. The only major downside with joining an affiliate network is that the fees for using their services can be quite high.

Affiliate Network Lingo

Affiliate networks offer merchants the ability to easily sell products, as well as allowing affiliates to promote and earn money. When you first learn about affiliate networks, marketing and related methods, the "lingo" and terminology used might be foreign and confusing.

It's important to understand that affiliate networks have different services, payment methods and revenue sharing options. Some affiliate networks only allow the sales and promotion of digital goods. Digital goods are also known as non-tangible items; including e-books, software and anything else that can be downloaded online. Physical tangible items are also sold and promoted through various affiliate networks. Some affiliate networks allow all of those items to be sold through the network, and others only allow one or the other.

The types of Revenue Sharing include: Cost per Click (CPC) or Cost per Sale (CPS). If signed up as an affiliate for a CPC program, then each time someone clicks on your affiliate banner or affiliate link, you will be paid (the amount is set by the vendor).

More commonly, CPS offers payments on a per-sale basis. So, if you are an affiliate for Honest Riches, you earn will be 50% of the total price after deducting the affiliate network's fees.

Recommended Affiliate Networks

New Affiliate Networks arise daily, so finding a credible, established and reputable program to join is important. Several have stood the test of time and have become well-known among many Internet Marketers.

Plimus
Website: http://honestholly.com/goto/plimus

- Affiliate Network with unparalleled customer support
- Advanced reports for affiliates and merchants, to track clicks, visitor statistics and amount of visits per sale (sales rate)
- Payments are sent out according to the user's preferences: check, direct deposit, Pay Pal or wire transfer

Clickbank

Website: http://honestholly.com/goto/clickbank

- Established Affiliate Network, selling digital goods only (e-books, software and other downloadable items)
- Payments are sent out every two-weeks (by check only)

Commission Junction (CJ)

Website: http://honestholly.com/goto/cj

- Well-known established affiliate network with a massive marketplace of items to choose from to promote
- The network sells tangible items as well as non-tangible items, such as e-books and software
- Payments are sent out according to the user's preferences, by check or direct deposit

PayDotCom

Website: http://honestholly.com/goto/paydotcom

- Another popular Affiliate Network
- Payments are accepted and sent out through Paypal (rather than by check)
- Affiliates receive their commissions monthly (rather than bi-monthly)
- Merchants have the ability to e-mail all affiliates individually or by mass mail

ShareASale

Website http://honestholly.com/goto/shareasale

- Major affiliate network with relationships established with businesses (merchants) as well as marketers (affiliates)
- Reliable payments, processing and support
- Huge array of companies to promote for, with banners, graphics and links to use in your websites or online

CHAPTER 3: FINDING AFFILIATE PROGRAMS

Think like a Consumer

Promoting products or services as an affiliate is an excellent way to profit online. First, do research online to know what type of product or service you would like to promote. Try to think like a consumer of the product you want to promote. For example, if you are considering being an affiliate for a company that sells herbal sleeping pills, then try to put yourself in the mindset of someone who might want to purchase that item. If you were that person, you would obviously have trouble getting a good night's sleep.

What websites would you turn to for advice, information or products? Why do you think you would prefer to buy herbal sleeping pills, versus over-the-counter sleep aids? Try to brainstorm and think like a consumer. Take time to peruse those websites and forums and see what products are currently popular. Go to the websites which offer those products, and see if the websites have affiliate programs.

Not all websites or businesses prefer to show a link to their affiliate program on the homepage of their website. This does not mean that an affiliate program does not exist, but it does mean that you may need to dig a little deeper to find it. First, look at the links on the top menu, then bottom menu – to see if there is a link that says "Affiliates" or a link that says "Partners."

If you cannot find one, then it may be wise to go to a search engine, type in the name of that website or product and the words "affiliate program." Most likely, you will have success in discovering if there is or is not an affiliate program. The research conducted above is quite basic, but it's important in the beginning stages of your promotional research and efforts. This is just to familiarize you with the process; the subsequent chapters will explain it in more depth.

> **Useful Tip:**
> Whether you are browsing the web with Internet Explorer, Firefox or an alternate browser, create a new folder in your Bookmarks Toolbar. You could name the folder: "Affiliate Programs". Through your research of affiliate programs, and when signing up, you can create Bookmarks to keep track of all the links. Personally, I have an Affiliates Bookmark Folder, then subfolders within it to specify in more detail what the sites are about.

Affiliate Networks vs. Independent Affiliate Programs

There are pros and cons to signing up with affiliate networks vs. independent affiliate programs. The table illustrates several major differences between the two types. This should assist you in your hunt for the ideal affiliate programs to promote.

Features	Affiliate Networks	Independent Affiliate Programs
Fees	Fee per sale, either a set amount (depending on the price of the item, or a percentage of the profits) – as high as 10%.	Generally do not charge a fee, and if a fee is placed per sale, it is often minimal.
Restrictions	Citizens of numerous countries are restricted from joining and receiving payments – due to complications with payment processors & banks (This may affect you if you are from a country in Africa or Asia).	Less restrictive and generally allows sign-ups from countries that major affiliate networks do not.
Payments	Payments to affiliates and merchants are generally consolidated – so you will receive your total amount of earnings in one lump sum.	If you are signed up with many different Independent Affiliate Programs, each separate program will be responsible for paying you at a certain time or when your earnings reach a certain amount.
Research	Researching affiliate programs in an affiliate network is quite simple. Most affiliate networks categorize their programs. or by keyword, makes your research easy.	Researching to find your ideal Independent Affiliate Program may require patience, as you will need to go from site to site to find out if there is an affiliate program. If you want to sign-up for multiple programs, you will need to go to multiple websites to conduct your research.

Overall, signing up with a combination of affiliate networks, as well as independent affiliate programs works well. Save the website addresses to your bookmarks folder, and keep track of you progress and earnings. Personally, I am a member of a wide variety of programs. I've learned what to look for in an affiliate program, from the standpoint of an affiliate and from the standpoint of a merchant.

For merchants who wish to have their own affiliate program, it's important that you do the research right away, before signing up and starting to have affiliates promote for you. I know this from first-hand experience. If you sign-up with an affiliate network, not knowing how high fees are and the restrictions for joiners, you will regret it later. You do not want to be in the position where you must move an entire empire of affiliates over to a new program, when they've already put in so much effort to promote for you and have their affiliate links all over the web.

Affiliate Networks for Global Entrepreneurs

Unfortunately, many affiliate networks don't allow people from countries outside of the U.S.A. and Europe to join. Hopefully this will change, so that payment processors and affiliate networks will be open to people globally. Until that ensues, those who are from countries that are restricted from joining must seek out independent affiliate programs to join. It may be a time-consuming task, but the research will be well worth it as you find the program that best suits your online interests (until more affiliate networks span out and allow more global residents to join).

Three affiliate networks that admit a wider scope of member registrations from countries all over the world include:

LinkShare
Website: http://honestholly.com/goto/linkshare

Kolimbo
Website: http://honestholly.com/goto/kolimbo

Plimus
Website: http://honestholly.com/goto/plimus

CHAPTER 4: AFFILIATE NETWORK CRITERIA

When researching Affiliate Networks, it's important to weigh out all your options and do your research thoroughly.

Affiliate Network Research – Questions to Ask

☑ **How many affiliate programs comprise this particular affiliate network?**

- If the affiliate network has several hundred affiliate programs, that means choosing items to promote may not be so difficult.

- This may also indicate how established this particular affiliate network is, or if it is fresh off the ground.

☑ **Which payment methods are offered & how often are payments sent?**

- PayPal, Direct Deposit, Check, Wire Transfers are examples of possible payment methods.

- Monthly and twice-monthly payments are common, although Affiliate Networks may also allow you to receive your payments based on a per-amount basis. When you reach "x" amount, your earnings are released.

☑ **What is the Refund Policy for buyers?**

- Numerous affiliate networks offer no-questions asked, immediate refunds guaranteed to anyone who purchases. In addition, the affiliate network may require merchants to agree to this policy, and state it on their sales page.

- To ensure customer satisfaction, having a 100% refund policy, is a good thing.

- The downside, with larger affiliate networks, is an increase in refunds (simply because people become aware of how "easy" it is to buy an item and get a refund). People who take advantage of the system, and chronically request refunds, may have their accounts suspended or closed (by the affiliate network), as what they are doing could be considered stealing.

- Affiliate networks may also allow the merchant who is selling their product to determine what the refund policy should be. That person may also be responsible for handling the requests and processing the refunds.

☑ **What are the payment processing fees?**

- Affiliate networks can charge fees of anywhere from 3% to 11% per sale (more or less). The amount is generally deducted from the total amount the merchant would earn, then after that the affiliates (if there are any) would receive their commissions.

- If you are a merchant selling a product, the percentage that you are charged per sale will add up quickly. This is of paramount importance for you to keep in mind prior to choosing a payment processor and/or affiliate network.

- If you are a merchant and your product sells well, you will end up paying a lot of money in payment processing fees (depending on which affiliate network you use).

So, if you have your own product that you want to sell, do your research before creating your affiliate program. My personal choice (after using all of the popular affiliate networks) is Plimus – as their customer support, advanced statistics & array of payment methods have been impressive.

CHAPTER 5: AFFILIATE LINKS & CLOAKING

Example Affiliate Links

Once you sign-up for a particular affiliate program to promote, the place in which you signed up with will give you a unique affiliate website address. That website address is the one you will use to promote that particular affiliate program.

> **Example of a Clickbank Affiliate Link (hoplink):**
> http://affiliate.publisher.hop.clickbank.net
>
> **General Affiliate Link Example:**
> http://websitename.com/?aid=123

Affiliate links are all setup differently according to the varying affiliate programs. Just be sure to double-check the link you are given before you post it or share it with anyone. Clickbank's affiliate links are referred to as "hoplinks." The affiliate ID would be the Clickbank affiliate ID assigned to the person promoting. To find the publisher's ID, login to Clickbank.

Then, click on the tab "Promote Products" and then "Marketplace." From the marketplace you can view all of the affiliate programs in the network. When looking at the affiliate programs list, you will see a short description, then details below it. There is a "create hoplink" link and if you click on that, you can insert in your affiliate ID – and it will output an affiliate link for you to use to promote that product.

Affiliate Link Cloaking

When you cloak a link, basically you are using a method to hide, alter or redirect the original link. Link cloaking is a common practice in Internet Marketing, for several reasons.

The more knowledgeable people become in Internet Marketing, the more aware people are of the fact that people might earn high commissions off of their purchases. Some people are disinterested in the "behind-the-scenes" process, others are totally unaware, and some people would prefer that no one gets a commission at all.

The people, who feel that affiliates should not earn commissions, generally try to change the affiliate link so you earn nothing from it. Unfortunately, this has become a common practice. The people who do this, either "cut off" part of the affiliate link so you (or whoever the affiliate is) does not get credit for it, or the person replaces your affiliate link with his own (so he makes a commission).

For example, let's say "John" is reading a very interesting and informative article about personal productivity. He is trying to manage his time more wisely. After reading the article, John sees that there is a link to personal productivity management software. When he scrolls over the link with his mouse, he sees the link looks like this: http://mannco.prodsoft.hop.clickbank.net.

John is a member and affiliate with Clickbank so he immediately recognizes the hoplink. John decides that the user "mannco" does not deserve to earn the commission off of his purchase, he would rather "steal" it and he replaces "mannco" with his user ID.

So, he recreates the link to look like this: http://john.prodsoft.hop.clickbank.net and he buys the software, and earns a 50% commission off of that sale (or 50% discount).

That is a typical example of how people can "steal" your affiliate commissions. It is why people choose to cloak links. When a link is cloaked properly, the viewer would be unable to do what John did in the example. The person would be unable to view the original link and therefore, would be unaware of the affiliate activity behind it.

Tutorial – Cloaking Affiliate Links with HTML

Link cloaking with HTML is a method which is not too difficult once you understand how it works. For example, let's pretend you want to write a product review for Honest Riches. You want the review to include a cloaked link to the Honest Riches sales page. For it to work, you need to have a website and web hosting. Just create a new html page and name it whatever you prefer (make sure it ends in either .htm or .html). Insert in the Link Cloaker HTML code below (replacing "http://youraffiliatelink.com" with correct details) – and save the page.

DETAILED EXAMPLE:

Your website address is: http://www.johnslifeonline.com. You create a page – honestriches.html and insert in the Link Cloaker HTML below (replacing the values with the correct information). Your cloaked link is: http://www.johnslifeonline.com/honestriches.html.

When clicked on, immediately the reader is actually redirected to your affiliate link website address. So, the viewer never sees an affiliate link, and if a purchase is made, you will earn your well-deserved commission.

Link Cloaker HTML

```
<html>
<head>
<title>Loading page...</title>
<meta http-equiv="refresh" content="2;URL=http://youraffiliatelink.com">
<script>
url='http://youraffiliatelink.com;
if(document.images) { top.location.replace(url); }
else { top.location.href=url; }
</script>
</head>
<body>Loading
<a href=http://youraffiliatelink.com>page</a>...
</body>
</html>
```

Recap

As per the example above, this page would be named "honestriches.html" and saved. After you write a review to the Honest Riches sales page – you can tell the reader that more information is available at: http://www.johnslifeonline.com/honestriches.html.

This is the cloaked link that will immediately redirect the user to your affiliate link. The same principle and techniques can be used for other affiliate programs (and you can name the page anything you prefer – as long as it ends with .htm or .html). Just replace the instances of http://youraffiliatelink.com with your actual affiliate link.

Tutorial: PHP link cloaking

PHP Link cloaking is another method to cloak links. The method differs from the HTML one because the code is shorter (and written in PHP).

☑ First - Create a Folder

The first step is to create folder on your website. Some people prefer to name it "go" or "visit," – the name you choose is entirely up to you. For example, if I want to cloak links for my website http://www.honestholly.com, this is what I would do. I would login to my CPanel (control panel with my hosting account).

I would then go into the file management area and create a folder. I would name the folder "go." So, on my site, the location of the folder would be here: http://www.honestholly.com/go/.

☑ Next - Create PHP Files

After creating the folder, you can then create your cloaked links. If you want to write a product review on Honest Riches and cloak the link, this is what you would need to do. First, go into the folder you created (the "go" or "visit" folder) and create a PHP file. You can use notepad or another text editor (or do it through the actual Cpanel). Make sure the file ends in ".php." So, if you create: "honestriches.php" – then you would only need to insert in this small snippet of code:

```
<? header("Location: http://youraffiliatelink.com"); ?>
```

☑ Finally - Save & Use the Cloaked Links

Then, save the file. If the example file, honestriches.php was saved to http://www.honestholly.com/go/ - then the actual cloaked link would be: http://www.honestholly.com/go/honestriches.php.

Anytime someone visits that website address, the cloaked link will immediately redirect the viewer to your affiliate link. For multiple URLs, this method is simple. Just login and go inside the folder you created, and add another small PHP file with the redirect code.

Link Cloaking Software

There are other alternatives, to cloaking links. Some of which might be easier to do, especially if you cloak a lot of links, or prefer to stay away from files and code. An excellent (free) link cloaker that can be used with Wordpress installations is the Link Cloaking Plug-in, created by Janis Elsts.

I personally use it with all of my Wordpress-based websites, and also have it pre-installed with the free websites I create for people at http://honestholly.com/goto/cheekyo. ✒

Anytime I want to cloak a link, I scroll over the "manage" tab in my Wordpress admin area, then click on "cloaked links." To cloak a link, you enter in the name of the link and the destination URL (this could be your affiliate link). For example, if I want to create a cloaked link to the affiliate network "cj" this is what I would do.

First, create a link name - "cj" is the name of my link and the destination URL is http://www.cj.com.

There is a link that says "show cloaked url," and when clicked upon, you would see this: http://www.honestholly.com/goto/cj. ✒

It's simple to cloak links with this plug-in. If you already have a Wordpress website, and would like to download the plug-in directly, you can do so through here: http://honestholly.com/goto/wpcloaker. ✒

Link Cloaking Precautions

When using your cloaked affiliate links online, be cautious in where you post them. Some websites allow the use of affiliate links in forum posts, for example, and others do not. Just be sure to read the rules and regulations on each website before you post the links. If you do not, other viewers might become upset with you or your account could become banned or restricted.

For full details about this, please refer to Book 3, Chapter 2.

Book 2

Research & Preparations

CHAPTER 1: PREPARATIONS

Visualize to Actualize

Preparing yourself and aligning your efforts to create a successful, sustainable income is the goal of this chapter. I will only touch on this subject briefly. Although it is important, the majority of this guide will be about the actualization of the entire process.

In order to achieve success with the system described, it's vital that you know exactly what you are trying to achieve. You must know precisely what you desire the outcome to be before you even start. This section will assist you in laying out a solid foundation to build upon. Subsequent books & chapters will describe the actual steps to complete your goals.

Try to clear your mind of all external thoughts and distractions for a moment and focus on one thing only. Visualize what you want.

Think about what your ideal life would be if you could be, do or have anything that you desire. Ponder your endless potential and possibilities. Think about the specific items that you want to have (for yourself, your business and your family).

Clear goal-setting is of paramount importance to your progress and success. Deterrents and distractions will arise everyday but if you know your goals and the steps to achieve those goals – you will find yourself with a clear path to follow. Unfortunately, some people quit before they even begin. Fear of failure and lack of success can hold a person back and keep that person from even taking a step in the direction of what they want.

Clearly Defined Goals

A goal is a precise, distinct, measurable state. Too often people confuse having a "direction" with having a goal. For example, someone may say that their goal is to increase their income. That is not a clearly defined executable goal. That is someone with a desire or idea. A specific goal is the destination. It is not the path or intention – it is the final point.

When I was 16 years old, my dream was to live overseas. All of my closest friends were from around the globe: Brazil, France and Japan. When I was in high school, I received a brochure one day in school that had information about being an exchange student.

Surprisingly enough, I was the only person in the entire school to inquire about it. I applied to take part in the Rotary Youth Exchange program to achieve my goal of living overseas. I completed an application, was interviewed on numerous occasions and I was awarded with the opportunity to participate in the program. I was thrilled.

At one point, I was given an option to tell the program operators which country I would prefer to be an exchange student in. Imagine being given a globe and choosing any place that your heart desires. I was excited as I received a very long list of countries, and I was required to number my choices (starting with #1, my first choice, and on through the list). I recall at that time, choosing Zimbabwe first, South Africa second, and numerous other exotic-sounding countries that I'd rarely heard of. In the end, I was sent to Bangkok, Thailand and I spent 6 months of my life there. It was an enriching and difficult experience to endure as a teenager.

What if I wasn't given that option to choose a country? Several of the countries on the list I was given had been experiencing instability in the country, fighting and hostility. I was surprised to see those countries on the list. What if they decided to send me to Iraq or Kuwait instead of Thailand?

Would my goal of "living overseas" have been accomplished? YES. But, in reality I would not have been happy if the exchange program would have sent me to an unstable country. My family would have been worried, and I would have been faced with a whole new world of challenges.

This example is to illustrate that a goal absolutely must be clearly defined and extremely specific. Goal-setting is one of the first steps you should take when getting started online. Be honest with yourself and explore what your goals are and what you are hoping will result from their attainment.

Creating specific detailed goals will allow you to measure progress. Understanding why you have that specific goal is of equal importance to the actual goal itself. If you know why you have that particular goal and what benefits you will receive from completing it, you will be driven and motivated to make things happen a lot faster. With no goals, you may find yourself distracted, searching the World Wide Web, chatting away in forums all day.

Writing your goals down, or using a word processor and printing out your goals so that they are visible to you on a daily basis – is also important. Waking up in the morning with a plan of action or vision clearly in mind will make sure each day of your life contributes to what you are striving for. Pictures can also help motivate a person. If your goal is to save up $2,000 USD within two months, to take your wife on a weekend getaway – hang up a picture of the destination. Put it in a place that will be visible to you and remind you of what you are working for.

Dream Boards

Creating a "dream board," can be a fun and inspirational project for you (and your family as well). If you are not interested in this, feel free to skip to the next chapter. For people who want to feel inspired, like when you were a child, let's continue.

When you were a child, do you remember having big dreams of becoming a doctor, an actor, or an astronaut? I know I did. I had my future mapped out when I was 14 years-old. I was going to be an ethologist specialised in primatology, living in the jungles of the Democratic Republic of Congo (formerly Zaire). My goal was to live among the apes (bonobo chimpanzees), study their behavioral traits and help the orphaned animals. They only have a 2% genetic difference from humans, and the main quality they lack (that we have) is the ability to vocalize their thoughts into speech in the ways that we use it.

I knew every single detail about the plight of the bonobo chimps, and even today I remember it all. I went to the Milwaukee County Zoo every weekend and every summer day. I was obsessed and some people may have thought I was crazy, but it was my passion. I applied to become a volunteer, but was not allowed to because I was too young. So, I went there on my own. After a lot of visits, the apes all knew me. It started out with one ape – Aliyah (a young 5-year-old). It's incredible what can happen in your life if you do something outside of the societal norms and follow your passion. I began bringing books and little toys, mirrors and key chains with me to show Aliyah and the others. Something amazing happened over time – all of the apes trusted me.

Whenever I arrived I'd just give Aliyah a certain glance and she'd meet me wherever I was standing. The exhibit there was very large and had many glass-plated windows which made up three of the four walls. You could be in close proximity (with a small piece of glass) in between if the apes would come to you (which they normally do not). Soon, very large groups of people would crowd around me as I showed Aliyah all the stuff I brought (especially in the summer months when the zoo was busy). I felt claustrophobic with the people around, and enjoyed the times there with just the apes. When the crowds grew, I would give Aliyah a little nod and glance and she'd run to the other side of the exhibit and meet me there. That soon turned into a game which comprised of her racing me across back and forth. I know people thought I was nuts, but they were also amazed by it all.

My family did not believe me, so I brought my big brother with me one day and he witnessed it all. I still have really good memories of those days of dreaming and of Aliyah. A year later, my family moved away and I couldn't visit often. Eventually Aliyah (and the rest of the group I knew) had passed away. My world changed, I began working a lot, and the dreams faded but were not forgotten.

Some people are raised with such strictness that they are scolded for dreaming big – and told to study hard to get their degree (in whatever field the parents push them towards). It is incredibly difficult to let go of all the conditioning that society and people have put on you – and truly open yourself up to learn and understand what you truly are passionate about. So, that's where "dream boards," come into the picture. They facilitate a way for you to be creative and let out that inner child, full of hopes and dreams (and no worries of money and bills). Not everyone is so passionate about their goals, and that is ok. A "dream board," will help you realize what truly makes you happy and what you want out of life – now and in the future. Basically, dream boards can be large or small. I prefer to use a white sturdy piece of art paper. You will need to have scissors, tape or glue. Look through magazines, newspapers, ads, or photos online. If something stands out to you – like a picture of a yacht or a sunset on an island (something that you would love to do, have or become) – then cut it out.

You can write on your dream board or just have it full of images. On my dream board I have pictures and I also wrote down names of people who have inspired me. Just having a photo of your child on the board can truly inspire you to do what you need to do to create the financial freedom you are striving for.

Quite a few psychological studies have been conducted on the topic of visualization (as a way to attain your goals). Some people believe that your brain cannot tell the difference between when you are visualizing something and when you are actually doing that thing. So, if you see and visualize yourself in your ideal situation (by letting yourself dream again or by looking at the "dream board" everyday) you can open yourself up to new possibilities.

CHAPTER 2: RESEARCH IS KEY

Plan of Action

The most crucial step (which so few people pay attention to) is conducting proper research before starting your venture online. Whether you decide to profit from non-website related methods or by having a website, you will need to brainstorm ideas, research and conduct a few tests before moving forward full speed.

If you skip this step or try to half complete your research in an effort to save time and make money right away – you may just end up setting yourself back in the long-term.

Conducting thorough research, having a plan of action and knowing exactly what you will do before you begin will save you time and help you to complete your tasks efficiently. The research methods explained in this chapter apply to you whether you want to have a website or plan to make money from only non-website related methods.

Although the thought of creating your own website may be overwhelming, fortunately it is possible for non-experienced users to do just that. Rapid changes in the online world have made it possible for anyone to create a website – you no longer need to be an HTML mastermind or have any elaborate skills. Keep an open mind as you learn more about the money-making options, which I will explain in the subsequent chapters.

Brainstorming

Now would be a good time to take a few minutes to write down some thoughts, interests and ideas. You can use the template on the following page or use a sheet of paper to brainstorm.

INTERESTS

_____
_____
_____
_____
_____
_____
_____

SKILLS

_____
_____
_____
_____
_____
_____
_____

IDEAS

_____
_____
_____
_____
_____
_____
_____

PASSIONS

_____
_____
_____
_____
_____
_____
_____

Trends & Ideas

When starting a venture online, some people discover that coming up with a clear idea to move forward with is easy. For others, it may be more arduous to find an idea to pursue. Using personal interests, ideas and ambitions and putting them into your plan of action can help drive your efforts. Thinking creatively, considering all options and being open-minded will help during the research phase.

Others (you know who you are) don't care what your venture is about as long as it is going to make you money. Believe it or not, it is possible to make money through internet marketing with an idea that you have no interest in personally. Some of the methods in subsequent chapters will explain how to do this. Start brainstorming by jotting down ideas, interests; what you think might be popular and profitable right now in the media or in society. And, although some products, trends or services might be in demand at the moment, it does not mean that you will make a load of money from the item or idea.

Keywords & Key Phrases

A key phrase (or more commonly known as a "keyword") is a word or phrase, which is typed into a search engine online. For example, when people go to Google and type in "buy golf clubs online" – that is a key phrase. The person is seeking to purchase golf clubs online. Your goal (if you were the webmaster or person selling golf clubs online) would be to have your website show up in the top 5 or top 10 list of websites that Google pulls up when that key phrase is typed in. In order to achieve the top ranking, you must understand how to conduct research and Search Engine Optimization (SEO). You will learn Search Engine Optimization in Book 5.

Target Market

Before beginning your research, keep in mind that you are trying to discover and analyze your target market. What is your target market group seeking to buy online? What keywords are being typed in the major search engines daily? What product or service might assist, benefit or aid your target market group?

CHAPTER 3: KEYWORD RESEARCH TOOLS

Using Online Tools to Find Niches

There are numerous online tools to help you discover exactly what people are searching for online every day and how many times per day. That type of information is vital, because it connects you with your target market.

It provides you with detailed statistics and information that you will use to find your niche, keywords and key phrases (if you are creating and optimizing a website) and possibly a new marketing idea. You will discover not only how to find niche keywords and key phrases, but how to find the most profitable ones.

Niches

What is a Niche? Even if you do not know what one is, you have most likely heard of niches and how profitable they can be with internet marketing. A niche is an idea or topic, which is very popular online, but which also does not have millions and millions of competing websites related to that topic.

Personally, I consider a niche when I check how many times a certain key phrase has been typed into Google in the past month. I look at that, and then I also check how many competing websites there are. If I see that there is less than 1,000,000 competing websites and the key phrase was searched for 200+ times per day then I'd say that's a niche.

Free Keyword Research Tools

There are several very useful, free research tools available online. They can provide you with keyword data, statistics and information about trends.

Trellian Free Software Tool
Website: http://honestholly.com/goto/trellian

Trellian offers a free online search tool to allow you to view statistical data of specific keywords or key phrases that are typed in. The free web-based version is extremely detailed and useful.

Trellian also offers a commercial version that has statistical data over a longer range of time, with more details and data.

Wordtracker's Free Software Tool

Website: http://honestholly.com/goto/freewordtracker

Wordtracker is an advanced software tool that continually collects, analyzes and categorizes words and phrases that people type into metacrawler search engines every day. A metacrawler search engine takes the search results from numerous other search engines and compiles and blends the list into one page.

An example of this is Dogpile. So when you do a search on Dogpile - the results are actually being retrieved from Google, Yahoo, MSN & AskJeeves. So Wordtracker gathers all the data from many different metacrawler search engines to put into its database of words. I've used Wordtracker in all of my past research projects for Internet Marketing. Wordtracker currently has a free research tool that can be used online. Personally, I prefer the free Trellian tool over the free Wordtracker tool.

If you have the funds and want to purchase a commercial version of either software, I recommend Wordtracker (although both are excellent). Wordtracker is well-known in the Industry and SEO firms as well as individuals use it daily to conduct keyword research and watch trends.

More Research Tools

Alexa.com (free)

Website: http://honestholly.com/goto/alexa

- Displays a link to view the most popular websites globally, according to: global 500, country, language or subject

Nichebot.com (free)

Website: http://honestholly.com/goto/nichebot

- Word trend Keyword Charts, Keyword Analysis, Keyword Projects
- File folders for project Management, Training center & articles for keyword research

RankPulse.com (free)

Website: http://honestholly.com/goto/rankpulse 📌

- Web tracking of Google's Top 1000 Keywords
- Database of keywords updated frequently, & allows browsing by topic or keywords to see what is most popular

Google Trends (free)

Website: http://honestholly.com/goto/googletrends 📌

- Shares data and keywords that the world is commonly searching for
- Displays the trends history, with the top cities, regions and languages

Cbengine.com (demo)

Website: http://honestholly.com/goto/cbengine 📌

- Software program which tracks Clickbank products sales rates & trends
- Shows which Clickbank products sales rates are going up or going down & by what specific percentage

Seasonal Ideas

The changing of the seasons can bring about many new opportunities to capitalize on. When Thanksgiving or Christmas is near, people are constantly searching for new recipes, different or unique gifts, greeting cards and other presents. You, as an Internet marketer, can take advantage of any or all seasons by researching and promoting what is "hot" or popular for a particular season or time of year.

Mass Media

Discovering what is "hot" and what is not is an easy task if you have a newspaper, tv or magazine. Advertisers are constantly creating new products, pushing technology to the limits, creating advanced toys, tools and gadgets. I've noticed, personally, that every time I turn the television on I see another ad for a new type of medication. It seems that new "diseases" are being discovered (or invented) every day.

With the new ailments come new products to help ease the pain for the person involved. Time-saving tools are created almost daily, which gives you an opportunity to take advantage of the popularity of a particular item or service by promoting it online as an affiliate.

Book 3

Profiting Without Websites

CHAPTER 1: PROFITING WITHOUT A WEBSITE

Testing Techniques

Many beginner Internet marketers feel more comfortable testing out several techniques through non-website related means when first starting out. This is a good way to break into the realm of internet marketing, acquire knowledge about the techniques being applied and start making money.

Honestly, I used to believe that profiting online through the non-website related means was less stable and may not create a long-term income. I've come a long way since I began my online endeavors, and I've learned that the non-website related methods can be highly profitable and sustainable. The non-website and website related methods to making money online both present different types of challenges and benefits – but both methods offer long-term income opportunities.

Real Example

For someone totally new to internet marketing, the concept of how to make money through these methods may not be totally understood. This is a true example of one method I have used to profit from affiliate marketing, with no website needed. I am purposely putting this before the rest of the chapter because it will open your eyes to the infinite possibilities, and hopefully motivate you to try out some of the techniques yourself. Following the example, explanations of exactly how to do this, as well as other related methods are provided.

Method Used: I promoted a product, using my affiliate link, on several public forums. I did not create a website and I used my actual affiliate links in my posts (I did not cloak them or hide them).

My Target Market: People who suffer from a specific health ailment which causes them pain, sleepiness and other problems throughout the day. (This is a niche group of people).

Affiliate Program: I signed up with an online pharmacy which sells a product that aids these people with their health issues. I have personally purchased this and vouch for it, as well as the pharmacy. (Never promote something you do not honestly stand behind). The online pharmacy gave me a personal affiliate link that could be used online to promote their products. Anytime someone clicks through my affiliate link, and makes a purchase, I then make a commission.

Commission Rate: The commission per sale is 15% recurring (for the life of the customer).

Action I Took: I found several online forums which were created to help people with this ailment. I wrote only a few short sentences (tactfully, as to not sound like my purpose was to spam them) and I included my affiliate link. One place in which I posted my short ad was at Topix.net – and it was never taken offline.

Example Ad: "I also suffer from BLANK condition and I found a reputable online pharmacy that I've been buying BLANK from. Here's the link:" http://www.affiliatelinkfromthepharmacy.com.

Advice: That example above is quite similar to the one I posted. I truthfully posted that as I had purchased from the pharmacy. I do not recommend that you lie and say you have tried something that you have not. Just be honest. If you just state that you've found something that looks like it might be worth checking into, that works fine as well. I've had the most success with extremely short posts. I also put the keywords I was targeting in the title of the post. I made the title similar to this "Cheap BLANK." (BLANK could be replaced with the name of the medicine).

Outcome: January 26, 2007 – I made my first three or four posts and then forgot about it, not realizing how profitable of a niche I had found at the time.

-As of May 28, 2008 I have made the Company: $64,009.85 in Sales
-I have earned $9,602.22 so far with my 15% commission rate
-Conversion Rate of 6.39% (and increasing gradually)

Why It Worked

Contrary to what so many people believe, topics that have nothing to do with working online and internet marketing can be tremendously profitable. This particular method (which required only a few simple posts or ads) has made me so much money and will continually increase, for several reasons:

☑ **Repeat Customers**

Any product which requires re-buying or a subscription to a service that is paid for monthly (or every few months for people buying medicine) will continue to pay. You must be signed up with an affiliate program that offers commissions on the lifetime of the customer, so when the customer re-buys or renews then you receive commissions each time.

☑ Search Engines

Prior to making the posts about the medicine, I did some keyword research. I had my keywords chosen and when I posted, I created a title which contained those keywords. Two of my posts were indexed by Google and several other search engines. So when people were searching for that particular product online, they would type in "Cheap BLANK" and my post came up at the top of the list. They clicked to read and eventually purchased through my link (after doing their research).

☑ Unique Niche

Lastly, this is a good niche because it is a product that people feel they need to have. It helps them personally, mentally and physically. It is a product that is very expensive if prescribed by a doctor, and many of the people could not afford it or were living in a country that did not sell it. I personally bought this medicine because it was totally unavailable in Thailand where I was living. (Advice: Abide by the laws in your country and online. When unsure, do your research and find the proper method).

Actual Screenshots of Earnings

Date	Sale Value (excl.)	Commission Rate	Affiliate Earnings (excl.)	Sale Status
05/19/2008	USD$349.00	15.00 %	USD$52.35	Pending
05/18/2008	USD$93.50	15.00 %	USD$14.03	Pending
05/17/2008	USD$93.50	15.00 %	USD$14.03	Pending
05/16/2008	USD$137.00	15.00 %	USD$20.55	Pending
05/16/2008	USD$85.00	15.00 %	USD$12.75	Pending
05/16/2008	USD$288.50	15.00 %	USD$43.28	Pending
05/14/2008	USD$269.00	15.00 %	USD$40.35	Processing
05/14/2008	USD$49.00	15.00 %	USD$7.35	Processing
05/14/2008	USD$262.00	15.00 %	USD$39.30	Processing
05/13/2008			USD$12.75	Processing
05/11/2008			USD$40.35	Processing
05/11/2008	USD$85.00	15.00 %	USD$12.75	Deleted (Admin)
05/11/2008	USD$85.00	15.00 %	USD$12.75	Processing
05/08/2008	USD$152.00	15.00 %	USD$22.80	Processing
05/07/2008	USD$162.00	15.00 %	USD$24.30	Processing
05/07/2008	USD$269.00	15.00 %	USD$40.35	Processing
05/06/2008	USD$93.50	15.00 %	USD$14.03	Processing
05/06/2008	USD$124.85	15.00 %	USD$18.73	Processing
05/05/2008	USD$162.00	15.00 %	USD$24.30	Processing
05/01/2008	USD$289.00	15.00 %	USD$43.35	Delivered

May 2008 Daily Sales Reports

Displaying 1 to 20 (of 475 sales)   Result Pages: 1 2 3 4 5 ... [Next >>]

Categories

The Affiliate Program

$64,009.85 DOLLARS in sales

(with only 6,632 Visits)
-15% Commission Rate
-$9,602.22 Commission for this Year

Welcome Holly Mann
Your Affiliate ID: 1

Affiliate Summary

Impressions: [?]	124	Visits: [?]	6632
Transactions: [?]	423	Conversion: [?]	6.38%
Sales Amount: [?]	USD$64,009.85	Sales Average: [?]	USD$151.32
Clickthrough Rate: [?]	USD$0.00	Pay Per Sale Rate: [?]	USD$0.00
Commission Rate: [?]	15.00%	Commission: [?]	USD$9,602.22

Click on [?] to see a description of each category.

Affiliate Summary

⇒ Edit Affiliate Account   ⇒ Newsletter

CHAPTER 2: FORUMS

Forum Profits

Millions of people congregate online everyday in forums, discussion groups or meeting places to address every topic imaginable. People always have questions and are on a never-ending search for answers and solutions to their ailments, worries and pains. This provides you an opportunity to join in and offer advice as well as subtly or tactfully promote a product or service. This is a cost-free method, and requires skill, which you will develop through trial and error. Your purpose is not to spam or provide false information or to push a product on anyone. The first step is to sign-up with an affiliate program that you would like to promote – something that you stand behind as a great product or service offered (and hopefully one which has a decent affiliate commission as well).

Once you sign-up for a particular affiliate program to promote, the place in which you signed up with will give you a unique affiliate website address. That website address is the one you will use to promote that particular affiliate program.

The second step is to find popular online forums or discussion groups that you can join. Be prepared and aware that although this method can make you money right away, it is a method, which should be used cautiously. Your purpose is not to join a forum and immediately post an affiliate link, telling people to buy a certain e-book or product. That will get you kicked out of the forum. A couple of years ago it would have been easier for you to get away with doing that and you probably could have made some quick money. These days it is considered spamming.

Participation & Posting

Now, if you would like to make money from forum posting, you should join the forum and participate in the discussions. You can create a signature, which will show up underneath your name in each post you make. And, in that signature you can create a link to your affiliate program. That way, every time you post, others will see your text/link underneath your signature. If they are interested or the text 'grabs' their attention, then they may click on it and purchase. This whole forum activity has been very profitable for me with several of my affiliate programs.

Most forums also have sections, which say, "Advertise Here," as the forum moderator may prefer to only allow advertisements or affiliate promotions in the advertisement section.

Rules are much more stringent in forums related to making money online, rather than forums related to specific interests, support groups or other non-marketing related groups.

You may be surprised, but if you are active member in an online community, the link in your signature will not go unnoticed & you should be able to make some cash from it. Not only can you make money from the forum visitors purchasing products through your link, but also from when the search engines pickup the posts. Then, people who find the site through doing research online may read your post and click through your link to make a purchase.

If you are having trouble finding forums related to your affiliate program of choice, just go to Google or another search engine and type in some phrases related to your affiliate program. Example: if I were to promote an e-book about "How to handle or deal with toddler temper tantrums," then I would type in phrases, such as:

- Toddler forum
- Parenting forum
- Parenting help forum
- Parenting support forum toddlers
- Toddler tantrums support

Before You Post Anything

Before you post a message in a forum, be sure to read the rules for that forum. Some forums do allow affiliate links, as others do not. Some forums are moderated to prevent posts, which are blatant advertisements, and some forums are not moderated and you can post ads freely.

☑ **Forum Netiquette**

Forum "netiquette" is a term that describes the standard protocol and manners to have while in public forums online. The netiquette will differ from forum to forum, but is generally specified in an agreement that defines the forum rules.

A potential user must agree to the rules when he/she is signing up to be a part of the forum. Unfortunately, people neglect the forum rules regularly, and post spam-type ads online repeatedly. The user must understand the forum rules before posting. Profiting from forums can be huge, but it takes a tactful person to do it.

☑ Trolls

Users who do not abide by forum netiquette are considered "trolls." These people are often repeat spammers, or people who create topics that are offensive and cause a stir in the forum. The posts are generally off-topic and not genuine, sometimes created with the intent to upset others. It is very unpleasant to be called a "troll," as I have encountered this in the past! So, take it easy when you first join a forum or discussion group – and get a feel for the environment and group.

☑ Forum Spam

Posting for the sole purpose of promoting a product, to make a quick profit, is considered forum spam. Some forum spammers have pre-written messages related to the forum topic. It may start out with a brief introduction, & then go into a message about how a particular product helped that person make money. If the forum rules allow this, then it is alright. If not – the person posting that message may be called a troll and their account might be deleted.

Attention-Grabbing Ads

You can post a short attention-grabbing ad (in the advertising section of the forum) to draw people in. You can then place a website link in your ad to your affiliate website. Example would be:

> "Urgent – must read report about Dog Training Tips that changed my dog and my life."
>
> For the free report, go to:
> http://mannco.websiteaddress.hop.clickbank.com (example affiliate website address).

When you place your ad, be sure to put the keywords you are targeting in the Title of the post. If people go to Google and type in "blank blank" (keywords) you would like your site to show up in the top 10 search results.

If you were targeting the key phrase "dog training tips," then the ad above would be acceptable, but it could be tweaked a little more. Whenever possible, put the key phrase you are targeting first, before the rest of the ad. You could rework the title above to say:

"Dog Training Tips: Urgent, Must Read Report that changed my dog and my life."

Creating Your Forum Signature

Creating a signature to use in forums is quite simple. The signature you create can consist of text that is hyperlinked or hyperlinked graphics. In general, forums use a type of code that differs from html – and is called BB Code. (BB stands for Bulletin Board). Let's say, I want my forum signature to look like the one below. I also want the words "Free Websites" to be hyperlinked to my website http://www.cheekyo.com.

Warm Regards,
Holly Mann
Free Websites

BB Code Necessary to Create a Signature that looks like the one above:

Warm Regards,
Holly Mann
[url=http://www.cheekyo.com]Free Websites[/url]

Creating Scripted-Style Graphic Signature

Another option is to create a scripted-style graphic signature (either comprised of just a graphic with a stylish signature on it, or with the graphic, text and hyperlinks). No experience is necessary to do this – no coding of html or BB is needed.

Go to http://honestholly.com/goto/mylivesig – choose from a variety of styles and colors. On the following page you can see an example of a graphic signature I created.

Blue Cursive

Holly Mann

Animate - Rename - Delete

Green Signature

Holly Beth Mann

Animate - Rename - Delete

After you create your signature, then you will have several options to choose from. You may either create a HTML-Signature or BB Coded signature. Using the free tool can save you time and increase your profits if used online and in forums.

Online Discussion Groups

You can also start your own group or community to reach others in your niche. If you choose a niche topic, it can be a great way to get a lot of like-minded individuals together. It can be a place to share information, promote products tactfully and share useful and helpful information.

Online Discussion Groups List

Yahoo's Groups
Website: http://honestholly.com/goto/yahoogroups

Google Groups
Website: http://honestholly.com/goto/googlegroups

MSN Groups
Website: http://honestholly.com/goto/msngroups

Live Journal
Website: http://honestholly.com/goto/livejournal

Groups are generally categorized according to different topics, and then subcategorized even further. Most websites allow regular users to join groups, as well as create their own groups. I created an interactive forum for the Honest Riches e-book buyers and myself to network, ask questions, share tips and help each other out. It's a big internet marketing family. It's a wonderful group of people who are generously sharing their knowledge with each other to help everyone succeed. My forum was created with Joomla, free-to-use web creation software which I explain in depth in a later chapter.

Honest Work From Home Forum
Website: http://honestholly.com/goto/honestforum

The purpose of online groups is to help people communicate through using the internet. It is free to create your own group and within minutes you can make announcement lists, mailing lists and public discussions. Having your own group through Yahoo Groups or Google Groups does not require you to have any knowledge in building a website (although it is the same as having one) and it is a good way to make money.

If you choose a niche topic, you can establish an important resource for people who are seeking information and support on that niche. You can have Google AdSense ads running down one side of the site (some groups allow this feature and some do not) providing more topic related information and you can also become an affiliate with a topic-related merchant to really cash in on the targeted traffic that your forum receives.

CHAPTER 3: WRITING

Writing Product Reviews

Another way to make money with little to no investing is by writing product reviews. Many people are making a living by only promoting products as an affiliate. This is a great way to start making money online – especially if you are in the process of developing a website or writing an e-book and you want to generate a decent income in the meantime.

But, you don't just want to promote any old product; you want to choose one that is "hot." There is a website called CBEngine. It is a software program that uncovers first-hand insider information about the Clickbank Marketplace products. It's like "insider-trading" so you can capitalize on the information and statistics. There is a trial version to use but several research features are unavailable unless you upgrade.

What the program does is tracks the Clickbank Product Sales Performance so you know that a product is finding a market.

It tells you the Clickbank products top "Movers & Shakers" which calculates Clickbank products with the most sales momentum. I have done extensive research on this and benefited from it greatly. I do research through CBEngine and write product reviews when I have spare time – which isn't often. So, from CBEngine you will discover which products are hot sellers – which ones have high numbers of sales and conversions.

In addition to knowing that, you should discover what the general public is typing in Google every day and searching for.

That's not the important thing though – you want to know the exact keywords and phrases, which are being typed in every search engine every day – and how many competing websites there are about that specific topic and how many people are paying for Google Adwords campaigns with those keyphrases.

Product Review Walk-through

Sign-up With Clickbank & CBEngine
- Sign Up With Clickbank– Open a Free Affiliate Account.
- Sign Up With CBEngine– or Use the Free Version Online.

Research Products of Interest
- Open up Microsoft Word or an alternate word processor and create a new document.
- Insert the website URLs of the CBEngine and Clickbank products you are interested in reviewing – with a side notes & details.

Go to Trellian's free online research tool.
- Look at your Microsoft Word document with the list of products and URLs. Type in the first product's name in Trellian's free online tool. The results which appear beneath the query will show you how many times that product was searched for, as well as other important statistics.
- You can also do the same Research with the Word Tracker tool. That way you can see if the product is gaining in popularity. If no one is searching for it, then move on to your next item.
- Next go to Google and type in the same product title. See how many websites show up. This is so you can see how many other reviews have been written about this product. You don't want your product review to blend in with the rest. You want it to stand out.

Decide Which Product to Write Review About
- You will need to purchase that product. Sometimes you need to spend a little money in order to make a lot in return.
- Technically, you are not required to buy it. But, if you are vouching for a program then it's a good idea to know the program first.

If you cannot afford to spend Any Money

- I'd recommend that you try to contact the creators of these products and present them with a professionally written e-mail explaining that you would like to write a product review for them and possibly promote their product.
- Then, they may give it to you for free. I advise you not to contact them until you already have a website with basic content on it. The e-book creator would trust giving away his/her product for free to someone who already has a website online (not someone who "might" create one in the future).

Write the Review

So, after using the product and analyzing the benefits and features, write your honest review. People do not like to read reviews which are 110% promoting the product because they may think you are only writing the review to make money from affiliate sales. Fortunately for you though, not everyone knows what an affiliate program is. In fact, many people don't know.

So when you write your review, be objective and write as a normal person explaining the benefits and what you've learned or what you have gained from it. I recommend that you list at least one thing that you did not like about the product. Otherwise it may not be believable.

Create a title for your review, which stands out from the other reviews about that product. The title should include the keywords you are targeting. If your review is about "Internet Millions," then make sure you include those words in the title. For example, "Internet Millions Review– Must READ before buying!" So, when someone types in "Internet Millions Review" into Google, ideally your review should show up. Make sure you put a link(s) to the product you are promoting in your article. You can say something similar to "Click here now to learn more."

☑ **Submit Your Review to free article sites online**

The purpose is to get targeted traffic and create links to your website (if you have one). Ideally, your post will get indexed by the search engines within a few days to a few weeks and have a high ranking.

SearchWarp
Website: http://honestholly.com/goto/searchwarp

GoArticles

Website: http://honestholly.com/goto/goarticles ✎

Article Alley

Website: http://honestholly.com/goto/articlealley ✎

Hot Lib

Website: http://honestholly.com/goto/hotlib ✎

Ideally, after about two weeks (sometimes sooner) – your review may be indexed by the Search Engines (that depends on the title you create, the amount of competing websites and other search engine factors which are sometimes unpredictable) – and you may start getting sales.

☑ **Login to Clickbank**

- Login to whichever affiliate center you are promoting to check your sales, conversions and statistics.

- The more article reviews you create, the more traffic you generate = more sales. I know this works because I have done it myself.

- I also know it works because my affiliates promote my product this way and get quite a few sales from it.

- You can also write reviews and create a website to post the reviews too. Blogs are easy to create and require no experience to setup (and it's entirely free) so that is a great option.

When writing a product review, so often I notice that people are writing their review just to make money from affiliate sales. That's fine and I recommend it – but only if it is a product you fully endorse.

People can tell if you are writing a "fake" review or one that you are promoting so highly & have nothing negative to say about it.

Even if you do love a product, try to add at least one piece of constructive criticism because it makes your review more real for those skeptics out there.

But I'm Not a Writer

If you're feeling concerned about how you write, there are always ways to improve your skills or work around the rough spots. If you plan to be successful working online (with any methods that you decide to use) you will need to put an effort into improving your writing skills. Bloggers make a lot of money blogging and writing every day, but it takes a little time to polish your writing so it is easy to understand, connects with the readers and is presented nicely.

Word Processing Software

Website: http://honestholly.com/goto/openoffice

First, it's important that you have decent word processing software to use. It is not vital, but helps greatly. If your computer does not have Microsoft Word installed, you can download Open Office for free. Open Office is a software suite for word processing. It is available in many languages and totally free to use for any purpose. It's a reliable product, offering users the ability to create advanced multimedia presentations, spreadsheets and databases. Open Office is the best free alternative to Microsoft Word.

Writer Resources

Copyblogger

Website: http://honestholly.com/goto/copyblogger

- Excellent resource to help you improve blog-writing
- Copywriting tips and resources

50 Tools to Improve Your Writing Skills

Website: http://honestholly.com/goto/50tools

- Clear concise writing tips to polish your skills
- Expert seasoned writers share tips, tricks and writing essentials

RhymeZone

Website: http://honestholly.com/goto/rhyme

- Just insert in a search term or phrase and view the definition, rhyme words, synonyms, antonyms, related words or quotes
- Must-have tool to improve vocabulary

American Writers & Artists Inc. (AWAI)

Website: http://honestholly.com/goto/awai

- Copywriting tips and strategies that can transform your income
- Free articles and affordable books available to improve your writing & sales

Copywriting Tricks of the Trade

If you are serious about improving your writing skills and are considering writing articles or even sales pages as a freelance writer, there are several resources to help you improve your skills quickly.

Personally, I have purchased "Copywriting Tricks of the Trade: 50 Essential Secrets That Every Copywriter should know." ($14.95 from the Awai Online bookstore). I downloaded it to my computer and printed it out to read it in my spare time. It helped me tremendously.

After purchasing, I was given a free bonus item, "The Art of Persuasion," which not only helped with my writing, but also in my personal life. I believe the company could have charged at least $20 dollars more for the information; it was of such value to me. The AWAI Website sells the book here: Website: http://honestholly.com/goto/awai

Quick Cash Freelancing

Writing articles is another way to make quick cash, while you are starting out. You can join a freelancer's website and create a profile. If you have written anything in the past, this will help, but it not necessary. Scriptlance is the website I prefer to use, to connect with freelancers.

Scriptlance
Website: http://honestholly.com/goto/scriptlance

After creating an account with Scriptlance, you can browse project listings. When individuals or businesses are in need of articles or content, they will post an ad with the project specifications, how much they are willing to pay, and amount of time they want it completed within. If you find the project suitable, you can "bid" on the project.

When you bid, what you are stating is that you are interested in completing the project and you would be best for the job.

You can state how much you want to get paid for your work (per article or per other specifications that you state). Sometimes the freelancers, who offer to complete the project for less money, receive the project.

I have hired freelancers to write articles and complete website design and programming tasks. I've also had software programs created for about one tenth of the price a normal programmer might ask for. When I have chosen freelance writers to complete a project for me, I have picked the person who sounded the most qualified and who can complete it in the least amount of time.

Generally, the freelance websites allow bidders and project creators to place comments on the project page. This allows the bidders to make a short statement about why he/she might be qualified to complete the project.

When I first began working online and needed extra money, I went on Scriptlance and joined the website as a freelancer. I saw a project posted by a man who needed articles related to military deployments, and how they affect family members. Since I was previously in the military and had experience with this topic, I bid on the project (and stated in the comment area that I am a U.S. Army Veteran).

 I was chosen for the project and completed it. I wrote several articles and earned a set amount per article (each was 400-600 words). I received 10-15USD per article, and it was much needed at that time.

It covered several startup costs that I incurred (buying a couple of domain names and hosting). It's a good option if you just need some really quick cash. If you are experienced in any other fields, like graphic design, those are other quick-cash freelance options. For more information about Scriptlance, please read Book 4, Chapter 3.

Accelerated Program for Six-Figure Copywriting

Writing content for your website and for sales letters is a tough task for anyone, with or without experience in the field. If you are struggling with your writing skills, and are interested in advancing those skills quickly (to help you in your Internet Marketing ventures and offline as well) – I recommend the Accelerated Program for Six-Figure Copywriting.

AWAI

Website: http://honestholly.com/goto/awai 📌

First, copywriting is a type of writing that is used to offer a product or service for sale. It is a promotional type of writing, used commonly in Internet Marketing. I've seen major Internet Marketers pay copywriters thousands of dollars to write "copy" for a simple sales page. So often I see sales letters that start with, "Dear Friend," and on to a big pitch that over exaggerates and under delivers in the end. That is not what the course is about.

The course is written by professionals in American Writers & Artists, Inc. (AWAI) and will legitimately improve your writing, sales and income if applied. If you want to become a copywriter (and earn a few thousand dollars per sales page) or if you just want to improve your writing skills to increase your revenue online – I would recommend this course. It is comprehensive, and for people who truly want to either drastically improve writing skills (specifically for sales copy), or for people who want to become copywriters.

You will learn how to craft a sales letter that sells, how to sell anything, the three fundamentals of selling, researching and understanding the buyer's profile, secret methods for establishing credibility, building an outline, grabbing your prospects, and the list goes on. You will become a true copywriter. Honestly, I have the course and I keep it on my desk, next to me at all times. It is an excellent reference point and I use it for all of my writing-related needs. If you want to improve your writing skills in any way at all, I recommend that you checkout the AWAI's bookstore online.

The resources are all priced reasonably, and every experience I have had with AWAI has been incredible. They over deliver with every single product and service. The resources are life and income-changing.

CHAPTER 4: SOCIAL NETWORKS

Social Networking Defined

Social networking is a term which defines a group of people online who collaborate for social or business reasons, in an interactive setting. Social networks can consist of groups of people who share similar ideas, or they can be large and varied in interests, sub-topics and groups. Social networking websites can dissolve barriers of distance, and create a setting in which others can "meet" and get to know each other online. Some people use social networking websites strictly as a social venue, to connect with old friends and family. Others use it with business in mind, to promote their services and reach the masses.

Joining Basics

Social Networks are generally free to join. Some require you to be of a specific age, and others do not. After creating a username and password, you can upload an image and edit your profile. There are usually groups or forums that you can either join or create – to gather with like-minded individuals. Many social networking websites give members a free webpage (that can be totally customized), free blog, galleries and other options to fully personalize it.

Social Network Niches

Social Networks are highly addictive for users. They are interactive and provide people with venues to join, share in and experience. Meeting new friends and business associates is rewarding. There is an increase in popularity of social networking sites online, and I believe this will only grow. Formats of social networks will become more interactive, useful & profitable for people. If you are interested in a particular niche topic, then joining a social network that relates to that topic is highly recommended. Understanding your niche market and becoming established online as an expert in that field, will create credibility for you.

List of Social Networking Websites

Social Network	Topic	Website Address
Bebo	General	http://honestholly.com/goto/bebo
BuzzNet	Pop Culture	http://honestholly.com/goto/buzznet
Care2	Social Activism	http://honestholly.com/goto/care2
ClassMates	School, College	http://honestholly.com/goto/classmates
Couchsurfing	Travelers	http://honestholly.com/goto/couch
Experience Project	Anonymous	http://honestholly.com/goto/experience
Facebook	General	http://honestholly.com/goto/face-book
LinkedIn	Business	http://honestholly.com/goto/linkedin
Meetup	Community	http://honestholly.com/goto/meetup
MyChurch	Christian	http://honestholly.com/goto/mychurch
MySpace	General	http://honestholly.com/goto/myspace
Ning	User-created	http://honestholly.com/goto/ning
Tribe	Create Tribes	http://honestholly.com/goto/tribe
WebBiographies	Genealogy	http://honestholly.com/goto/webbios

CHAPTER 5: WEB 2.0 MOVEMENT

Definition & Benefits

Web 2.0 is a phrase or term which has been used loosely to describe websites which are generally created by a community of users. Web 2.0 websites are interactive and allow people to become content creators and authors. The benefits from joining a website that allows you to become a content creator are vast.

First, joining a website and publishing content to it, not only establishes a level of expertise for yourself, but it creates an online presence (that you may not have otherwise had). Not everyone can afford to purchase a domain name and hosting. If you are in that situation, joining and producing your content on a Web 2.0 interactive, user-based website is an excellent option.

Even if you do have a website, adding content elsewhere will greatly increase your reach online, website traffic and your search engine ranking.

Two examples of user-created communities are Squidoo and Hubpages. Both of these websites are extremely popular online, and have authority in the major search engines. By "authority," I mean – the pages that are created by individual users tend to gain a high search engine ranking (quite quickly after creation). This means, if you join these websites and create some useful content, Google and the other major search engines will most likely index it. You will then receive traffic and if you have utilized the monetization tools – make money as well.

Squidoo & Your First Lens

Website: http://honestholly.com/goto/squidoo 📌

Squidoo is a highly interactive website, comprised of content created by the public. You can join the website for free, and then build your first "lens." A lens is a term used to refer to your squidoo web page(s). Each time you want to write about a specific topic, you create a lens. It is one full page packed full of information about that topic.

A lens can contain videos, RSS Feeds, links to outside websites (great for SEO), Amazon Books, Flickr photos, opt-in boxes (to build your list) and much more. You can write product reviews, give your opinion on a topic, and use all of the tools to monetize.

Reasons for Usage

- Market your business or promote affiliate programs
- Establish your presence online
- Create links to your main website/SEO

Hubpages

Website: http://honestholly.com/goto/hubpages 📌

Hubpages is another community created by the contributions of individuals. It is interactive, and provides an array of profitable monetization tools for you. When you join, you will be given the option to incorporate your Google Adsense account into your profile and hubpages.

This is important because Google Adsense provides you with an opportunity to profit from placing content-relevant ads on your websites. Hubpages gives you the option to allow the ads to be placed on your hubpages. This way, you can earn money from your hubpages (and Hubpages would keep part of the profits).

For someone who cannot afford webhosting and to have their own website, this is a great way to make money (with no start-up costs).

CHAPTER 6: E-MAIL MARKETING

Definition & Purpose

E-mail marketing encompasses tactics which webmasters or marketers use to correspond with possible clients, website visitors and subscribers. Contact is based on electronic mail (e-mail or auto responders). Examples of e-mail marketing include: newsletters and subscriber opt-in boxes.

It is a powerful method that is extremely profitable, if you are tactful and provide excellent resources to those who subscribe.

Automatic email responders are special email addresses that return a pre-stored message or set of messages in response to any email sent to the auto responder address. You can set an auto responder to send the first message immediately, then after X number of days you can have another message sent out, then after X more days.

Basically, subscribers are those who sign-up (provide an e-mail address, first name and possibly more details) by filling out a simple form on your website. An opt-in box is a simple box and short form that allows a visitor to sign-up through.

A double opt-in is a term which refers to someone who signs up, then is required to verify the sign-up as well. Generally, an e-mail is sent to the person who signed up, immediately after the sign-up. The e-mail will thank the person for signing up and ask the person to click on a special link to verify that he is the one who signed up, before it is confirmed.

The double opt-ins is very important because they are people who sincerely want the information you are providing. They have taken the time to specifically click and verify that they want to be on your list.

E-mail marketing software allows you to create numerous lists. You might have a list for people who have joined a specific newsletter, a list for people who want a particular article or download, and other lists for follow-up.

The more specific and organized you are, the more you will be able to test your results, and reach the right people (in turn, profit more).

Building Relationships

Creating relationships is the core of e-mail marketing. If your goal is to make quick cash, it will be abundantly clear to the subscribers on your list. They will most likely delete your message before they even open it. Then they will unsubscribe from your list.

Think about the purpose before you create your e-mail messages. It is normal to want to make money from an e-mail message, but it is more important that you provide something of value to your readers. The money will come later.

The most important part of the process is building trust, creating a lasting relationship and providing value.

To be safe, I recommend that you refrain from "selling" or promoting anything in the first two to three e-mails you send in a particular campaign. So, if you have created a series of four messages which contain information about a certain topic, do not promote or sell anything until you reach the fourth message.

You can create all of the messages prior to putting the campaign online. You can create the first message to be sent immediately after the sign-up happens. The other messages can be sent out at different dates (example, several days after the first message is sent out) and the fourth message could include a promo. Patience can be profitable in this situation.

Avoiding Trouble with E-mail Marketing

First, do not ever, under any circumstances, spam your subscribers. It helps to put a disclaimer or short note to potential subscribers, that you will not use their e-mail address in any other way than to contact them with whatever information that was requested. Make it clear that you will not sell or rent out their information, and that you are against spam.

If you are ever accused of spamming people, your e-mail accounts could be closed down, and even your hosting account (and possibly your websites as well). It is a serious offense, and in some countries it is even illegal. So, be careful.

Avoid Using Certain Words

When sending messages or e-mails, take caution in your choice of words. Certain words will automatically trigger the e-mail service to block your message or filter it directly into the spam or bulk mail folder. It's difficult to successfully get your message across, when so often the words that you want to use will trigger spam-filters to discard your message. So, for the responsible e-mail marketers, your job just became tougher. You need to learn how to delicately write your newsletter, while watching out for the filters and still getting your message across clearly.

☑ Simple Trick to Circumvent Spam Filters

An easy way to use the word that you prefer to use in your e-mail message is to alter it slightly so that it is not triggered as a spam word. The problem is that spam filters are so advanced, it is difficult to know what is acceptable to do and what is going to trigger the filters. In any case, many internet marketers tend to use this simple tactic to avoid the spam filters.

If they want to use the word "free" in their headline or message, they do not spell it out as mentioned previously. Rather, they might write it with an asterisk in the word somewhere. Free might become f*ree or fr*ee. Personally, I think it looks tacky, but it seems to do the job. I tend to use the words "at no cost" or "no cost to you," instead of typing f*ree. Sometimes my messages are filtered into the spam box, but more often they are not.

☑ Spam Triggers List

All New	Get Paid	Satisfaction
Avoid Bankruptcy	Guaranteed	Serious Cash
As Seen On...	Great offer	Subscribe
Call now!	Giving it away	Time limited
Cash	One time	Unsecured debt
Discount	Online pharmacy	While Supplies last
Money	Order Now	Work at home
Free		

Auto Responder Software

Finding decent auto responder software to use is one of the most important decisions you will make with your internet marketing career. It is a choice which will impact you financially (and in turn, mentally) because if you choose the wrong one, or find that you are unhappy (after already paying for something) you will lose money and may have a very difficult time transferring over data to new software. I am writing that out of personal experience.

I purchased auto responder software in the past because a friend (who I admired online, and clearly knows his stuff) recommended it. It was not overly user-friendly, and after using it for a while, I built up a list of over 10,000 people. One day, I attempted to login through the administration area, and saw that it was deleted.

I am unsure if someone hacked into my site and deleted it, or if something else occurred. But, it was all lost. Thankfully, I had a backup of my database, which saved all my past clients information.

That situation forced me to do more thorough research to find better, more suitable auto responder software. And, thankfully I found something that I am extremely happy with. It is user-friendly and it is affordable (only pay for it one time and use it forever). It has advanced statistics so that you can track what is working, how many people have viewed your messages, where the people are from geographically, and more.

I've heard several major affiliate marketers promote auto responder software to others. 95% of the time, they have endorsed auto responder software which requires you to pay monthly for the use of it. I nearly signed up for one of those services, but thankfully I avoided that. Anything that requires you to pay for monthly will become extremely costly to you long-term. So, the major affiliate marketers who were promoting those auto responder services were looking out more for their wallets, rather than yours.

From the standpoint of a person who is starting out, and needs real honest guidance, the best option is to go with software that requires a one-time payment. Once you sign-up for the month-to-month payments (which so many auto responders require), you will be stuck with that company for a long time. It may be extremely difficult to change or transfer any subscribers over to a new server or software program.

Interspire SendStudio – E-mail Marketer
Website: http://honestholly.com/goto/sendstudio

The auto responder software I prefer to use is Interspire's E-mail Marketer (previously known as SendStudio). Once purchased, you can either install the software yourself (to your website) or pay a small fee to have someone with Interspire install it for you.

Personally, I installed the software myself on a sub domain of one of my sites. Example: www.domain.com/news/. I used CuteFTP to upload the files to my website and install SendStudio.

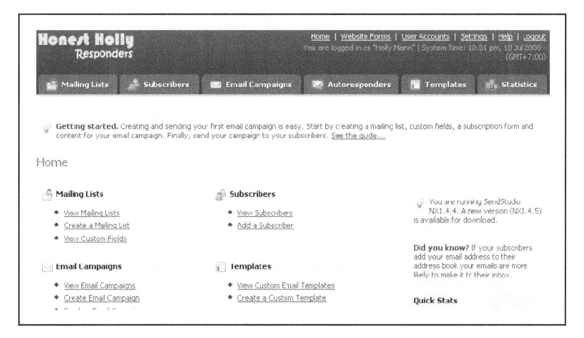

Send Studio's User Area

The screenshot above shows what you will see after you login to your administration area. The newest version of E-mail Marketer will differ slightly in appearance and have additional features. I also "branded," or added my own logo to the software, to personalize it for my e-mail marketing campaigns (that is free to do).

The price for Interspire Email Marketer for one user is $249 USD (please note that the price may change at any time, and you should check the website for accurate details).

That could be a lot of money to someone who is just starting out. Interspire also offers Email Marketer for 5 Users for the price of $439 USD. If you can get a group of 5 people to split the cost of the software, you could all benefit from having it, and each pay only $88 USD. The important thing is that you pay for this software only one time, and can use it forever. There is also free customer support for 3 months, and quite a few guides for usage.

After it is downloaded, you will also see that you receive "tips" to increase the amount of times people open the e-mails you send and in turn, how to increase profits with e-mail marketing.

An alternative (for someone who would prefer to pay monthly and avoid installation) is to use Interspire's hosted plan. The pricing structure varies, but for less than $20 USD per month, you can send up to 500 e-mails.

The software makes it simple to view, edit and create mailing lists and campaigns. If you are starting fresh, and have a website, the first thing you will want to do is create a new mailing list. After you create the mailing list, then create a website form for that list. Once the form is created, you can take the code and put it into your website wherever you want the form to appear. That's it. It's quite simple to do, but takes more time and effort to create multiple follow-up messages.

It's important that you try to be as consistent as possible, with sending out regular messages (if you want to truly captivate readers and keep them interested). It is not an easy task, but if you are focused and are passionate about the topic, it will be easier for you to do.

Features Include:
- Custom Field creation allows you to personalize the e-mails.
- Professionally designed e-mail templates are included and have been tested to work with all e-mail clients.
- It's easy to add your own logo, text and color scheme to truly brand your e-mail marketing experience.
- For each campaign, you can see exactly how many people opened their e-mail, how many people unsubscribed, which links they clicked, e-mail forwarding statistics and more.

Prospects, Personalization & Profits

Personalizing your e-mail messages, will increase your rate of success with e-mail marketing significantly. If you see that you have a message in your inbox, and it starts out with, "Dear friend," "Hey," or "Hey you," would you open it? Most likely you would delete it. If you can personalize the user's experience, and at least say "Dear Jane," or dear "whatever their name is," then it will make quite a difference.

Book 4

Website Creation

CHAPTER 1: WEBSITE DESIGN OPTIONS

Web Design Options Overview

By this stage, you may decide that you would like to have your own website. If you are unsure about how to go about doing this, don't worry. There are ways that you can set up a free website yourself - even as a beginner. Or, if you really think you do not have the time or skills to do this, you can hire a designer to do it for you for a reasonable price.

In this chapter, you will learn about the different website design and development options. It's difficult to keep up with the ever-changing web design sector of the Internet. I am constantly learning, expanding and testing out new software and programs. Technology has changed so drastically over the past several years. The Internet has become a place in which even the most inexperienced person can create a stunning website.

This chapter will teach you about the basic options to choose from for your web design and development. Subsequent chapters will take a deeper look into utilizing the different options by going further in detail for each one.

Website Requirements

The first thing you must understand when you are considering having your own website is that you will incur several costs (although there are cost-free options which I will also explain in this chapter).

☑ Domain Name

A domain name (also known as: hostname, URL or website address) identifies your website, and is generally purchased through an accredited domain name registrar online. The price per domain name varies, but in generally is around $6-20 USD per year. The basic purpose of a domain name is to create a memorable name for your website, which is used in place of its numeric identifier (IP Address).

☑ IP Addresses

IP Address stands for Internet Protocol Address. For example: 72.29.89.134 is an IP Address. Each machine that is connected to the Internet has a clearly defined set IP Address. You can think of it like street addresses, but for computers. I would prefer not to cause too much confusion on this topic, so I will leave the description at that.

For further information about IP Addresses, hostnames and domains – please refer to: http://honestholly.com/goto/ipwiki. ☝

☑ **Website Hosting**

In order to make your website accessible, viewable and live online, you will need to pay for website hosting. Basically, what you are paying for with website hosting is a space on a web hosting company's server, which includes Internet Connectivity and File Uploads (to your website or websites). The features of different hosting companies vary considerably. I have multiple web hosting accounts personally, and I prefer and recommend BlueHost: http://honestholly.com/goto/bluehost. ☝

The price is $6.95-8.95 per month, and allows you to add multiple domain names to your account and host all domains with one plan. So if you were to purchase several domain names and want all of those domains to be hosted on one single plan, it is not a problem. Choosing the right domain name and web hosting company are important steps in setting you on the right track with your website.

☑ **When researching different hosting companies, check:**

- Price (per month or per year)
- Server Uptime (reliability of the company and server)
- Customer Service (24 hour support, online help, toll-free number)
- Company History (age of the company, how established is it)
- Features (compare features and see if multiple sites can be hosted on one account)
- Reviews (read real customer reviews before buying)

Traditional Website Design

When I began my Internet venture online, I created my first website through what I would consider to be "traditional website design methods." I used a website design editor (Microsoft FrontPage) to create my websites. I'm informing you of this, so you realize the major downside to website development in the manner I did it, and how to do it more efficiently.

This section will help you to use a few smart fixes to avoid the tedious tasks that kept me busy for hours on end, while I could have been focusing on other projects. If reading this section causes you to feel extremely overwhelmed or tense with the thought of creating a website in this manner, please feel free to come back to it at a later time.

I recommend that you skip over to Chapter 2: Content Management Systems (CMS). It is the method of website design that I recommend (and prefer to use). The information in this chapter is specifically for people who want to know about traditional website design options and tips.

My Experiences with Traditional Website Design

With minimal website design experience, I started out by creating an index.html file. Your index.html, index.htm or index.php is generally the file that is used as your default homepage. When people navigate to your website, the first page they will see is this page.

So, I created my website from a template which I found online for free. Everything seemed fine, and I started to create content for the site. Every single page I created, I did in the same manner. In the program, there were two viewing screens: one which showed the actual html code and one which showed the actual design that I could edit on screen. That screen is commonly referred to as a WYSIWYG editing screen. WYSIWYG stands for "What You See Is What You Get."

Within a couple of weeks, my website grew quite large. Early on, I copied my original template index file and saved it as blank.html. Then each time I added a page, I copied the code from blank.html and put it in a new file, edited it and added my article to it. Experienced web designers reading this will be laughing to themselves at my silly methods.

Not only was I actually not saving time by doing that, but with each page added, I was creating a whole load of extra work for myself. What do you think I did when I needed to change the links on my website?

The simple change should only take minutes, but it actually took me hours to do. It required that I copy the item or code that I had changed, then open up every single html file in my website and manually edit and save each one. Sometimes I would accidently miss a page here or miss a page there, and the website quickly became disorganized and sloppy.

Advice for Beginners

For beginners, I honestly don't recommend that you start out by creating a website in this manner. If you find yourself feeling totally lost and overwhelmed while reading this chapter, feel free to skip it and move onto the next. If you decide to venture into this at a later date, the information is here as well as online (in more depth and in tutorials). For now, I recommend that you use a Content Management System (CMS). A CMS-based website has an administration area that you can login to so you may easily add content anytime. If you would like to change the menus or links, you can do it one time and the change will take place throughout the site on every page. There is no need to immerse yourself in html code, because the site is already setup for you and designs can be changed easily. As mentioned earlier, feel free to skip right over to Chapter 2: Content Management Systems (CMS).

CoffeeCup HTML Editor

Website: http://honestholly.com/goto/coffeecuphtml 📌

For those who feel inclined to learn by using the traditional website design methods, there are several software options to choose from. I prefer to use CoffeeCup HTML Editor. I have tried out and tested numerous others, but have found that the features and stability of this software to be the best.

The software price (as of 2008) is: $49 USD with a 30-day free trial. The software has been the most popularly downloaded HTML-editing software online since 1996. It has a visual editor, code editor and a split-screen (if you are interested in learning the coding behind the design). I highly prefer this software to all others that I have tried.

For those who are lacking in funds, or who really want to become comfortable before committing to purchasing, there is a CoffeeCup Free HTML Editor as well. It is a drag and drop HTML editor with Built-in FTP uploading. It has wizards for frames, forms, fonts, tables and a quick start to help you create web sites fast. According to the website, it is a "trimmed down version" of the CoffeeCup HTML Editor.

HTML Explained

Hyper Text Markup Language (HTML) is a popular and widely used "markup language" for web pages. The files either end with a .htm or .html. Using an HTML-Editor will allow you to create HTML (or PHP-based) websites. The following information is designed to give you a basic understanding of a simple HTML page, its elements and how it is put together. If you use CoffeeCup HTML Editor, for example, all of the required HTML basics for your pages will be built-in. You will not be required to hand-code or insert in the document type and other attributes. Working with the actual HTML code is optional, as it has a visual design area for you to drag and drop and add elements.

☑ **Document Type**

Each page should start out with a piece of code which explains the type of document it is. This is a standard, and basically tells the browser what you have created.

```
<!DOCTYPE html PUBLIC "-//W3C//DTD XHTML 1.0 Strict//EN"
"http://www.w3.org/TR/xhtml1/DTD/xhtml1-strict.dtd">
```

☑ **Opening & Closing Tags**

Each individual page will contain an opening tag and a closing tag.

Opening Tag: <html> Closing Tag: </html>

☑ **Body Tags**

All the information or content between the opening and closing tags will be enclosed within a body tag.

Content Opening Tag: <body> Content Closing Tag: </body>

Full HTML Page Code Example

```
<!DOCTYPE html PUBLIC "-//W3C//DTD XHTML 1.0 Strict//EN"
"http://www.w3.org/TR/xhtml1/DTD/xhtml1-strict.dtd">

<html>
<body>
This is where all of your page content goes.
</body>
</html>
```

(Just save your file as index.html or index.htm and view what you just created. It is a simple and quick start to having your own html website).

PHP Explained

Equally popular with HTML, PHP Hypertext Preprocessor (PHP) is also commonly used. Not only does it reduce the time needed to create large websites, but it also creates a more interactive and customized user experience. Interactivity through forums, e-commerce shopping carts & help desks and so much more can be done through PHP. Organization is vital to successfully managing your website. I recommend you create several files and folders when you first start.

- Index.php (this is your home page)
- /images (this is an images folder)
- /css (this is a folder which will contain your style sheets)
- Robots.txt (important file providing info to the search engines)

To avoid all of the tedious tasks that I created for myself when I began, you should begin by mentally or visually laying out your website. In addition to the files mentioned above, I recommend that you create several others to "call into" your homepage.

- Header.php (contains the top of your page, possibly an image or logo)
- Navigation.php (file which contains your menu bar)
- Sidebar.php (text or links that you have on the side of your page)
- Content.php (the main content area)
- Footer.php (bottom text in footer, copyright)

Think about your website Index.php file as the homepage, the place that will "call in" all the other elements. This will allow you to have a handful of files that are being included into your homepage to create your website. If a change needs to be made to the navigation or menu bar, you would only need to open up the Navigation.php file, edit it to your liking and save it. The changes will take place site-wide. To include the outside files within your Index.php file, it is rather simple if you are using PHP files (rather than an index.html file).

Useful Tip:
The files do not need to be named Sidebar.php, Content.php, and Footer.php as mentioned above. It is an example, and you may choose to name the files anything you prefer.

PHP Design Mockup

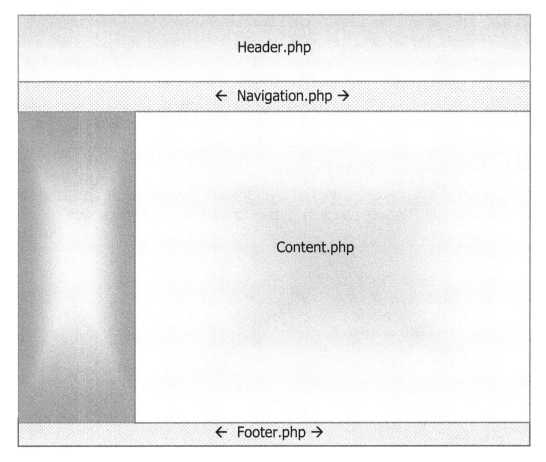

PHP Functions

As a total beginner to PHP, it's important to know that the PHP scripting language uses functions. The one function you need to know, as it is the biggest time-saver, is the "Include" function. The "Include" function is what you will use to create a website with a similar layout to the one in the figure on the previous page. Within the Index.php file, you want to include the Header.php, Navigation.php, Sidebar.php, Content.php and Footer.php.

PHP Include Function

The PHP Include function is a small piece of code that you use when you want to include one file within another. It helps to think of the elements on the homepage of your website as all separate files. When including other files, just be sure to have those other files created and saved. The example code below is assuming that I have already created a Header.php file (which contains possibly a logo image or header text) and that I have created a Navigation.php file which contains the menu links. This method will save a lot of space on your index.php file, as well as save time in recreating each page every time a change needs to be made. If you want to change the menu, just open up your Navigation.php file and edit away. The changes will take place site-wide.

PHP Include Function Code Example

The example below, shows how you can easily include any external file into your current one (through the PHP include function). It is much easier than it may sound.

```
<html>
<body>
<?php include("Header.php"); ?>
<?php include("Navigation.php"); ?>

<p>Welcome to my Homepage!</p>

</body>
</html>
```

PHP Tutorials

Website: http://honestholly.com/goto/phpbuilder

CHAPTER 2: CONTENT MANAGEMENT SYSTEMS

Basics of CMS Websites

Content Management Systems (CMS) give you the ability to add, update & edit your site without needing an HTML editor or software to do so. CMS sites allow you the flexibility & control to have an advanced, professional, database-driven website which is fully editable through an administration panel online.

Features of CMS Websites

The features and capabilities are endless. You can edit, add text, articles, news, photos and more through an administration panel on your website. You do not need to know html or have any website design experience. I have tested out numerous CMS platforms online and have found the most advanced features, style and ease of use with two of them, Joomla (formerly known as Mambo) and Wordpress.

Joomla

Joomla is a well-known and popular CMS. Once your website is installed and running, it is simple for even non-technical users to add or edit content, update images, and to manage the critical data that makes your company or organization go. It may involve some learning and adapting to the administration panel, but once you are familiar with it, it's a breeze. Via a simple, browser-based interface you will be able to easily add new press releases or news items, manage staff pages, job listings, product images, and create an unlimited amount of sections or content pages on your site.

Features of Joomla Websites Include:

- E-commerce and shopping cart engines
- Forums and chat software & image galleries & form builders
- Directory services & E-mail Newsletters
- Banner advertising systems & subscription services

Several Examples of My Joomla Websites
Honest Forum

Website: http://honestholly.com/goto/honestforum

Mannco Designs

Website: http://honestholly.com/goto/mannco 📌

Internet Millions Review

Website: http://honestholly.com/goto/imreview 📌

Wordpress Websites & Blogs

Wordpress is a CMS with an array of features, fully-editable through an admin area, and may be used as a blog or as a static site. A blog is a web page maintained and updated regularly with news, information, images and other media. Blog posts are generally displayed in reverse-chronological order (with the most recent entries on the top), and site visitors can comment on posts and interact with the writer as well as other readers. On the other hand, a static site consists of a homepage (that stays the same), lists of pages, as well as posts which may fall under certain categories. The main difference is that the homepage does not contain a reverse-chronologic listing of most recent posts.

Free Wordpress Blog

To get a free blog with Wordpress, just go to wordpress.com, sign-up and within minutes you will be setting up your new site. Creating a blog (even free ones) can be highly profitable, although there are several downsides to the free blogs. Wordpress.com's free blogs have domain names that are long and not overly professional. For example: http://example.wordpress.com (as opposed to a totally unique domain name, http://www.honestholly.com).

Wordpress.com is basically paying for your web hosting when you have a free Wordpress site, and because of this, certain features are not allowed with your free website. Google Adsense, Yahoo Ads and other similarly related advertising methods are prohibited. If possible, my recommendation is to purchase a domain name and website hosting, rather than use the free Wordpress blog. If you aren't ready for your own website yet, then feel free to explore options that are free. Don't worry about not having the choice to put ads on your free blog, because you can still profit in the long run.

After conducting thorough research, you can start to add content to your blog. You can gain a high ranking, your website will be seen in the search engines as an authoritative quality site, and you can always purchase a domain name or hosting later.

Wordpress Website with Hosting

Using Wordpress as your website's platform, with a purchased domain and web hosting is an excellent option for a first website. It's also a great option for someone who has created several websites through traditional web design methods. To clarify, Wordpress.com allows people to do one of two things. First – a user can sign-up and create blogs for free.

When the user logs into their blog admin area, they are actually logging into the Wordpress.com website, then into their personal website admin area. The free sites are hosted by Wordpress.com, and features are slightly limited. Second, a user can go to Wordpress.com and download the actual source files (in a zip format) so that the website can be setup and installed and owned fully by them. This would require a domain name and website hosting only. The files installed will be the basic Wordpress platform, with a couple simple features built-in. You can upload and add additional features at any time.

Advantages to Hosting Wordpress Websites

- Fast loading when hosted separately. If your website is a free blog that is hosted on the Wordpress server, then there are thousands, if not millions of others who are hosting on there as well. You will notice a big difference in loading time with separate hosting.
- Full capabilities to optimize your site for the search engines. You can insert header, description and meta tags to each individual page (I believe this is of extreme importance).
- You can choose and upload as many different themes as you like – with a click of a button through the hosting company.
- Putting Adsense Ads and other profitable affiliate marketing related ads on your website can be done only if you have separate hosting.

Feature-Packed Free Website

I've setup a service to offer all Honest Riches buyers the opportunity to have their own professionally designed website setup (by me and my programmer). It is based on Wordpress, but drastically differs from the basic setup.

Cheekyo Free Website

Website: http://honestholly.com/goto/cheekyo

The normal admin area with Wordpress-based websites is difficult to use and not pleasing to the eye. I've recreated it, offering drop down menus full of options and features all built-in. When a person uses Wordpress, it comes pre-installed with only a couple simple features. Then, you can add additional features, which are called "plug-ins," to increase the range and options with your blog or website. The problem with this is that the normal user may not know how to add files, upload and install plug-ins.

The average user may not be familiar with doing any of it – so I've setup your website for you with all of the best plug-ins already pre-installed. There is no need for you to do any of that. It is a time-consuming task that should be left to the programmers, not the users.

You will have an easy-to-use Admin Panel that allows you to add, edit and change all of the functions, features, links, text, photos and ads. It is FULLY Customizable by you in the administration panel. You also have a wide variety of professionally designed website templates to choose from. With the click of a button, your site's entire design will change and that does not interfere with all of the text and links you have already added.

COST: $0 – FREE

The website is created with Wordpress, but it contains all of the best plug-ins, features and themes. This will save you time, save you the hassle of needing to go into your file management area and upload items.

Features Include:

- Advanced Contact Forms (You can create as many as needed)
- Photo Galleries (Create galleries, albums and upload images)
- Write Posts or Pages and manage placement of each

- Easy drag-and-drop sidebar management (this allows you to move around elements that will show up on the side of the page)
- Google Adsense Ads integration
- Banner Ads Management
- SEO All-In-One Plug-in – each page or post will have an option at the bottom of the screen for you to insert in a custom Title, Meta Tags and Description (unbelievably important to get your website to a higher ranking)
- Huge assortment professionally designed Themes (designs) to choose from & use
- Website statistics and Google Analytics integration

To view screenshots of the features and your website admin area, please visit: http://honestholly.com/goto/cheekyoscreenshots. ✎ The templates or Wordpress themes

that are available to you can all be viewed here:
http://honestholly.com/goto/cheekyothemes.

The website is pre-installed with 24 of the most stunning themes I have ever seen. When logged into your website admin area, to change a theme or the website design, just scroll over "design," and click on "themes." What is the Catch? I do have one requirement and that is you use web hosting through a specific affiliated web-hosting provider, Bluehost.

Bluehost

Website: http://honestholly.com/goto/bluehosthr

BlueHost's hosting network meets the minimum wordpress hosting requirements (MySQL database and PHP and Cpanel). Bluehost will also provide you with one free domain name, which is included in the price of your hosting purchase. It is extremely important that you have your website hosted separately so that you can create a professional business website that is fully optimizable in order to attain high search engine ranking.

Your website will have unlimited features (non-hosted Wordpress websites are more restricted with plug-ins and links). Bluehost also allows that you host multiple domains on one hosting plan (if you have more domains, you can add them and have more sites – but the price is the same).

In order for you to be eligible for your free website, I only require that you sign-up for web hosting here: http://honestholly.com/goto/bluehosthr.

Once you sign-up, then all you need to do is forward me the welcome e-mail which should contain website details and account login info. You can either fill out the form on the Cheekyo website, or send it directly to me through my helpdesk here: http://honestholly.com/goto/supportdesk.

I will then work with my web programmer to get your site installed and up and running ASAP. I will e-mail you with your Admin Panel Login details. It sometimes takes 24 hours for your domain name to "resolve" and become functional. We will monitor that and set your website up at the earliest available time (within 5-7 days, usually sooner). Then you're set and you will have your own website. If this is not an option for you, due to lack of finances – then the next best option for the time-being would be to create a free blog. Also, establish your presence online through hubpages and squidoo.

More Free CMS Websites

Using CMS platforms to build highly interactive websites is increasing in popularity daily. The different types of CMS platforms vary according to features. Here is a list of several of the major, well-established CMS Platforms available.

Geeklog

Website: http://honestholly.com/goto/geeklog - Geeklog is a CMS Platform with features that are similar to Wordpress.

Zen Cart

Website: http://honestholly.com/goto/zencart - Zen Cart is a free CMS Platform that can be used for e-commerce purposes. The creators of the software are store shop owners, programmers and consultants.

PhpBB

Website: http://honestholly.com/goto/phpbb - PhpBB is a free forum CMS Platform, which is well-established online.

Moodle

Website: http://honestholly.com/goto/moodle - Moodle is a well-established and popular CMS for educators and students. It is a course management system for educators to create and hold online learning programs.

To compare CMS Platforms, please check out the comprehensive list here: http://honestholly.com/goto/opensourcecms.

CHAPTER 3: HIRING A DESIGNER

Affordable Freelancers

If you would prefer to have someone else setup your site for you, then you can hire a freelance website designer or programmer to create a website for you. You can have the designer create the website to your exact specifications, needs and desires.

In order to have your website produced, you will need to come up with a website plan or outline for what you would like created. Once you have the outline or site plan organized, then you will need a website designer. Website design generally costs in the price range from $20-$5000.00 dollars (more or less) and it's difficult to know who to choose and which companies you can rely on to deliver the best results.

If you want a high-quality website, designed to your standards and specifications, try Scriptlance. When I don't have time to design a website, I pay someone on Scriptlance $20-60 to create one for me. Scriptlance is a website which connects professional freelance website designers, programmers, graphic designers, software developers, and search engine specialists & writers with business owners, entrepreneurs and people like you and I.

Scriptlance
Website: http://honestholly.com/goto/scriptlance ✈

Whenever I need a website to be designed or programmed (and I just don't have time to do it myself), I go to Scriptlance. I have found so many highly professional, talented programmers and designers to build/develop automated sites for me that I find myself using it quite a bit.

☑ **It's free to post projects - which specify:**
- Your website design and/or programming needs
- Your approximate budget for the entire project & timescale

☑ **Project Bids**

Then Freelancers will place bids – offering you their services for a certain price and telling you how long it will take them to complete the project. This could be within a day, 3 days, a week, a month - depending on the complexity of the project.

They may place messages on a message board for you and you can correspond before choosing a person. Check out their feedback rating before choosing as well. But, I have found that some Scriptlance "Newbies" will complete your site design/project for practically nothing because they are starting out and want feedback. It's worth a try.

You do not pay until you are satisfied. You can deposit your money via Paypal (or another secure payment processor) into Scriptlance's account area. From the secure account area you can escrow the payment to the programmer. This enables the programmer to see that you have the funds to pay them and that you intend to do so provided the work is completed to your satisfaction. You do not need to release the payment to the programmer until you are completely satisfied with the end result. That way you are protected during the whole project process.

☑ Lacking in Funds

If you are lacking in funds and you have a great idea that you think might make you thousands of dollars - just post the project and see how much the bids are. Scriptlance has been a lifesaver for me. I am a creative person with new ideas all the time - imagine if you could tell someone your idea and have a software program created out of it.

When I first started working online I stumbled upon Scriptlance. I didn't have any start-up money but I had a great idea for a software program to assist Mortgage and Loan officers to keep track of leads. Sounds simple but it is much more complicated of a project than that because I wanted it to be completely automated so I didn't have to do anything at all and the program could be resold many times. After posting the project and waiting a few hours I checked and there were several bids: all of which were above $3,000. USD.

I did not have the money so I sent messages to all the bidders thanking them for their bids but letting them know that I could not afford it - and I asked them if they would be interested in sharing the proceeds of the sales with me indefinitely for creating this software program for free. Someone may very well be willing to create something for you for free in exchange for a percentage of the profits. I think it's a great deal. If you are going to do something like that just make sure that you have all your bases covered and a really thorough contract.

You can view and copy or use my contract template (with the names and personal information xxxxx out) so in case you do something like this you will have something to work from. The file is available at: http://honestholly.com/goto/examplecontract

CHAPTER 4: WEBSITE DESIGN RESOURCES

Website Design Lingo

☑ **Domain Name**

A unique name that identifies one or more IP addresses. For example, the domain name abacus.ca represents one IP address. Domain names are used in URLs to identify particular Web pages. Every web site that you visit is stored under domain name.

☑ **Flash**

Browser independent vector and graphic animation technology owned by Macromedia Inc. Most browsers support Flash technology and one flash animation looks the same on all browsers.

☑ **FTP**

FTP stands for File Transfer Protocol which is one of the methods of transferring files over the Internet.

☑ **GIF**

GIF stands for graphics interchange format, it is a bit-mapped graphics file format used by the World Wide Web. GIF images are limited to 256 colors.

☑ **Hosting**

Hosting is a service provided by hosting company. That's a place (a computer available on the Internet) where web site is stored and made available to web site users to view the content of that web site.

☑ **HTML**

HyperText Markup Language, the authoring and editing language used to create web pages on the World Wide Web.

☑ **JPEG (JPG)**

Stands for Joint Photographic Experts Group. JPEG uses compression technique for color images and therefore some details are lost in the compression yet giving relatively good quality. It is widely used on the Internet and other digital applications.

☑ Link (aka Hyperlink)

A link is object on the web page. When visitor of a web site click with the mouse on that object then user is taken to another web page where the link is pointing to. Different types of links are: text links, graphic links, java links, form links and some other which are not very important.

☑ PHP

PHP Hypertext Preprocessor is a server-side, HTML embedded scripting language used to create dynamic Web pages. Designed for Windows and Unix type platforms.

☑ SEO (Search Engine Optimization)

Search Engine Optimization (SEO) is a process of increasing site visitors to a web site, through a range of strategic methods. The methods include: linking, keyword usage, content and on and off-site optimization tactics.

Website Design Resources

Web Design from Scratch

Website: http://honestholly.com/goto/webtutorials ✈

- Comprehensive resources for website design, web 2.0 information, the design process, graphics, etc.
- Excellent resources for people who want to increase web design knowledge and learn to apply all the techniques

Web Developer Notes

Website: http://honestholly.com/goto/webdev ✈

- Web design basics to the advanced
- Tutorials, tips and tricks of web design

CHAPTER 5: UNDERSTANDING RSS

In the old days of Internet Marketing, just bookmarking websites worked well. But, when you bookmark a site, you must search through the site itself to find all the new content. If you subscribe to RSS, you will be notified of new content for that particular site, in an organized way. Short summaries and a link to the post will be provided.

RSS Defined

RSS stands for "really simple syndication." It is a way for you to stay updated with all of the new content on a website, without having to search through the site to find it yourself. If you enjoy reading online, it basically saves you the time of having to dig around a website for past posts. This way, you can view the RSS feed for a website, and only click to read more of what interests you.

RSS Feed generally consists of a list of recent posts (by date) with the title of the post, summary and link to it. In order to manage all of your feeds and subscriptions, feed readers can be utilized.

Feed Readers

A feed reader is a program used to help you organize all of your website feed subscriptions. It helps you to keep your feeds organized so you can easily browse through them and read whatever you want to read. Personally, I prefer to use Google's Reader. If you already have a free Google Account, then you can login using your Google Account details and start using the Google Reader.

Finding & Adding RSS Feeds

When using a feed reader, at some point you will need to insert your feed URLs. That way, the feeds can be tracked and added to your feed reader list. Most feed readers allow you to create categories or tag your feeds, so they stay organized.

I created numerous categories for my feeds, including: software, productivity tools, work from home, internet marketing news, and friend's feeds. So, after logging into my feed reader, I can click on whichever category I am interested in browsing feeds for.

When browsing websites online, it's generally quite easy to discover if the website has an RSS feed you can subscribe to. The site may have a text link somewhere which says,

"Subscribe to RSS," or it may contain a small image, such as:

If you are using the Google Reader to manage your feeds, then you can easily add the feed to your reader. Scroll over the small RSS icon or the actual hyperlink that says, "Subscribe to reader," or "Subscribe to RSS," and right click with your mouse. Then you can either click "copy link location," or "properties." If you click "properties," then a popup window will show you the full RSS URL. Copy the RSS URL and login to your reader to add the RSS feed to it.

E-Mail Subscriptions

If you prefer to receive e-mail notifications when a website makes a post, you can do that as well. It may be easier for someone who is not familiar with their feed reader yet. On http://www.honestholly.com for example, I have the option for readers to subscribe via e-mail notifications. So, whenever my website is updated with new content, they will receive a short e-mail summary and link to the article posted. I prefer this method over reading through the feed reader.

Website Owners

If you are a website owner, and you want to provide an RSS feed to your readers, you can do that easily with Wordpress or Joomla. A feed is automatically built-into your website if you build it through a CMS. You can also monetize your feed; manage subscriptions and tracking for free with Feedburner. Feedburner offers website owners the ability to manage all of their feeds in one place. If you have multiple websites, this will help you save time and earn more money.

Feedburner

Website: http://honestholly.com/goto/feedburner

Feedburner is free to join. After joining, you can add feeds and "burn" them. I'll explain what this means and how to do it. First, login to your Feedburner account. Assuming you already have a website, you will then click on "My Feeds." You will be brought to a page which will let you burn feeds. If you are unsure of the exact feed URL of your website, then you can insert the website address instead.

If the website has a valid feed already, then the next page will allow you to insert a feed title and create the link to your new feed. That's all it takes and Feedburner will provide you with your new feed link. The purpose of burning your feeds with Feedburner is because the website offers an array of features to manage your feed and profit.

Features & Benefits:

- Track visitor statistics & subscribers – just like managing your own list
- Monetize your feed with Google Adsense ads incorporated into them
- Optimize the way your feed looks; change colors & fonts
- Easily create widgets or subscribe boxes to place into your website to allow users to sign-up for your feed

RSS Confusion

If you are still confused about RSS and feeds, there is an excellent resource at: http://honestholly.com/goto/feedinfo.

Book 5

Search Engine Optimization

CHAPTER 1: SEARCH ENGINE OPTIMIZATION

Purpose of SEO

The purpose of optimizing your website is so that search engines can easily search your site, navigate through it and categorize it. As well as creating a graphically appealing, informative site for your visitors, you need to concentrate on building a strong keyword-based theme throughout the site.

Search Engines Defined

Search engines are large databases of websites that are automatically generated. These Internet search engines use a software robot or spider that seeks out and indexes websites. Yahoo, Google, MSN, Excite, AltaVista and AskJeeves are examples of some of the most popular search engines. To produce accurate search results, search engines must keep their ranking algorithms (formulas) secret.

Overview of Process

The process of SEO begins with choosing your keywords (based on research conducted to find your target market). This is the most important step, and Wordtracker (and several other free search tools online) can be used to do this. This is an important first-step and goes hand-in-hand with developing your website theme and choosing a domain name.

While choosing your key phrases, you should check out your competing websites. You cannot optimize your website to reach its highest position without understanding exactly how your competitors' websites reached theirs.

Do not move onto the next step in the process without totally solidifying the keywords and key phrases that your website will be based upon. You cannot move confidently in the direction of optimizing your website without this being set in stone.

Begin with the end in mind – and everything you do after this is based upon this step. All supporting articles and content for the website will be based upon these particular keywords and key phrases. The next step is to gather material for your website and put it all together so it is graphically appealing, not only for site visitors but for search engines as well.

This step may take quite a lot of time, and is usually ongoing. It is important to continually add, edit, and update your site. Every piece of text you add to your website should be supporting the site's overall theme.

Getting Indexed Right Away

Once you have your website completed, you will want Google and the other search engines to start indexing your web pages. In the past, people used to submit websites to the search engines, but from a SEO perspective, this is no longer advised.

According to numerous online search engine specialists, manually submitting your website to Google and Yahoo can sometimes cause a delay in search engines indexing your website.

The sure way to get your website indexed and listed in the search engines quickly is by having another website link to yours. Established websites are being crawled by search engine spiders regularly and the link to your site will drive the spider to index yours as well.

The higher the ranking of the website that links to yours, the quicker your website might be indexed. If you manage to get a link from a PR 8 website to yours, your site should be indexed within 24 to 48 hours.

For the rest of us, it generally takes a couple of weeks to have your site "grabbed" by a spider and placed anywhere on the search engine, but it may take more or less time depending on the website and the search engine. Even after it does have some type of ranking on the search engine, it may still be pages and pages deep.

CHAPTER 2: SEO RESEARCH EXAMPLE

Example: Website for Parents of Multiples (SEO Steps)

Let's say that I want to create a website about being a parent of multiples. I have a personal interest in this topic because my brother and his wife had triplets. Before I go out and buy a domain name and hosting and start throwing a website together, I'd take a few notes and do some serious keyword research.

Target Market:
Parents of twins, triplets and multiples and their family and friends

Service to Provide:
Resources, information, articles, advice and links to more resources

Profitability:
I will profit from placing Google Adsense Ads and other banners on the website, as well as by linking to products through my affiliate programs (Amazon.com and Cj.com). I will also create a product at Cafepress (custom designed "Proud Parent of Multiples" shirts to sell).

Possible Keywords:
Here I will do multiple searches on Google based on possible keywords and key phrases related to the topic. The number to the left of the keyword or key phrases represents the approximate number of competing websites for that particular term. (Please note: This information changes daily and will vary)

- 462,000 for "parent of multiples"
- 894,000 for "parent of multiples advice"
- 7,620,000 for "articles parents multiples"
- 628,000 for "triplets clothing"

Trellian's Free Research Tool Results:

First, I insert a broad search term related to "multiples." This brings up related terms that have been typed into the search engines over the past month, as well as number of times per month.

"Multiples" has been searched for nearly 4000 times in the past month, so I decide to check out how many competing websites there currently are in Google for that keyword. I type "multiples," (without the quotes) into the Google Search Engine and find that there are: 44,000,000+ competing websites. I decide to narrow it down into more of a niche or related keywords.

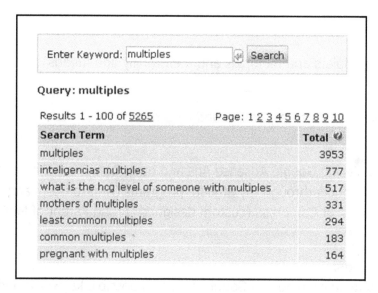

Trellian's Free Keyword Research Tool Results

Narrowing Down the Search:

I conduct more research and discover that "parents multiples," shows a less significant amount of traffic, but more about what I am interested in at this point.

The reason is because if I can reach the top ranking for a handful of related key phrases (which are narrowed down from the main keyword), then as time passes I can add more content to reach more competitive key phrases. I type "parents multiples," (without the quotes) into the Google Search Engine and find that there are: 500,000+ competing websites (much less than the first search).

This seems more than feasible for me to gain a top ranking for these keywords.

Additional research also shows me that there are searches conducted related to clothing for multiples, clothing for twins, and clothing for triplets – all opportunities to increase profits for my website.

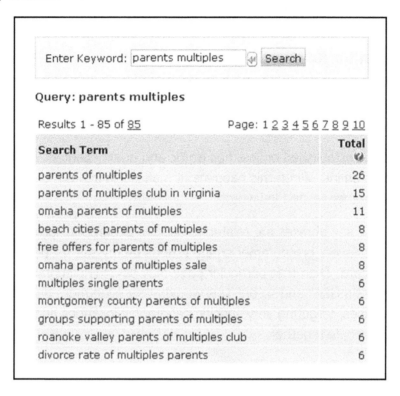

Enter Keyword: parents multiples ▾ Search

Query: parents multiples

Results 1 - 85 of 85   Page: 1 2 3 4 5 6 7 8 9 10

Search Term	Total
parents of multiples	26
parents of multiples club in virginia	15
omaha parents of multiples	11
beach cities parents of multiples	8
free offers for parents of multiples	8
omaha parents of multiples sale	8
multiples single parents	6
montgomery county parents of multiples	6
groups supporting parents of multiples	6
roanoke valley parents of multiples club	6
divorce rate of multiples parents	6

"Parents Multiples" Trellian Results

Short Term Goal & Keywords

I've decided to create my website and optimize it for these keywords:

Main Keywords
Parents of multiples
Parents multiples

Supporting Keywords
Multiples single parents
Groups supporting parents of multiples
Support parents with multiples
Pregnant with multiples

The supporting keywords listed above are going to be kept in mind, while I am mainly optimizing my website for the key phrases "parents of multiples" and "parents multiples."

This will be possible because I will create a lot of content, articles and resources which all contain the same theme – "parents of multiples," and everything related to being a parent of a multiple. I will also create articles with very specific key phrases in the titles, related to all my supported keywords listed above.

Long Term Plan for Keywords

Once my website is at a top ranking for "parents of multiples" and "multiples parents," then I will keep it there for a while before branching off further into creating a lot of content related to some other keywords (ones that have much more competition).

Once the website is established online, has traffic and quality content, it will build in ranking and status online. When this happens, it makes it much easier to gain an even higher ranking for other related keywords.

Since several of the key phrases are related to specific geographic locations of triplets groups, I may just have a programmer create listings on my site for people to join and list their city and state. Then that particular page may say, "Triplets families in Milwaukee, Wisconsin USA" and so on. This would allow even more pages to be indexed by the search engines, targeting very specific geographic locations and groups, while connecting these people together.

CHAPTER 3: SEO IN DEPTH

My Experiences

Within the past few years of working online I have created more than 150 websites through a variety of methods. The process for me has become methodical and I continually adapt it as I see fit according to the search engines and changing technology. The techniques I will list for you, step-by-step are the exact same ones I use every time I create and fully optimize a website.

To this day, every single niche website I have optimized for specific keywords or phrases has reached top ranking in the search engines.

The truth is, the term "SEO" frightens a lot of people and it can seem like too big of a hurdle to overcome. It is not, and by creating your first niche site and having it reach a high ranking in the search engines – you will know what to do to continue the success with other websites.

The potential success that you can have will depend on a variety of factors: the keyword(s) you are targeting, the amount of competing websites you have, whether you follow all the SEO steps and other uncontrollable search engine factors.

If you would like to view how many competing websites there are for a particular key phrase then type the keywords on Google and/or Yahoo.

If your website's topic is about "Texas Hold'em Poker Strategy", (this is just an example - this key phrase has a huge amount of competition), then strive to get as many high-quality articles with the words "poker" and "strategy" and "Poker Strategy" and add the articles to your website.

It might take you a few months (or much longer) to get any placement. In that case, you may want to choose keywords that are slightly different, for example, "poker" and "tips" and "poker tips", if those keywords have less competition.

Changing one keyword can make a difference of millions of competing sites and save you so much time.

Step-By-Step SEO Guide

☑ **Conduct Keyword Research**

- Conduct basic keyword research by typing into Google, analyzing competing websites and using the free keyword research tools listed in the previous chapter.

- Choose the keyword(s) or phrases you would like to create a website about and optimize for. These are tentatively going to be the keywords you use, as you need to do additional research before finalizing them.

Competing Websites Check in Google

☑ **Analyze Your Competition**

- Know how many competing websites you have for the keywords you are targeting.

- Check the number of back links your main competing websites have by going to Google and typing: link:http://www.websiteaddressofyourcompetition.com (A list of websites which contain a link to that one will show up.)

- This will tell you which sites your competitors are linking to, so you can link to the same ones.

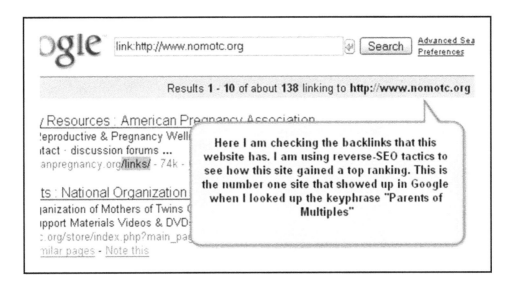

Backlinks Check

☑ **Create Document & List Outgoing Links**

- Open up a text document and paste in the website addresses of the places where your main competing website has links in (these are usually directory websites or link exchanges on websites)

- At a later time, you too can submit to those same places (and more)

☑ **View Linking Strategies of Competitors**

- Analyze your main competing websites outgoing links to see if that website is connected through many domains: http://honestholly.com/goto/siteadvisor. ✄

- This information can tell you if your goal in beating out this website is feasible or if the website has a network of established websites which are all high ranking (which means it could be a tough one to beat).

Checking a Website's Linking Strategies

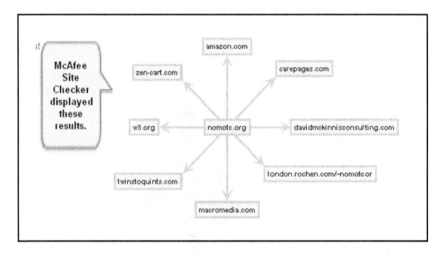

Viewing the Linking Strategies

The two screenshots above show what I saw after typing in the main competitor's website address in McAfee's Site checker. First I was told that there were no problems with the site – no spam-related content known.

Next, I scrolled down and was shown all of the links coming from the site I entered in. If I were to actually create a website about "parents of multiples" then I can see which websites have helped my competitor reach a high ranking. I know that twinstoquints.com could be a possible link exchange partner.

☑ **Way Back Machine**

Go to the Way Back Machine: http://honestholly.com/goto/wayback 📌 to discover the history of your competing website(s), when the site was established, how many pages it contained and how it progressed. This will reveal a lot of specific website details so you know how they reached such a high level in the search engines - helping you do the same thing.

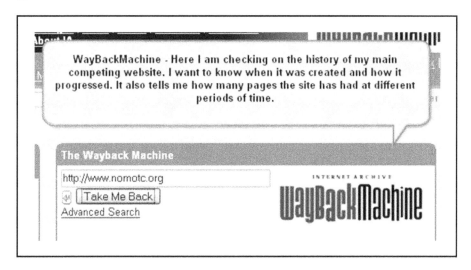

Way Back Machine

☑ **Finalize Keywords & Create Website Plan**

- After thorough research (in the previous steps) you can now finalize your choice of keywords to target for your website.
- Be specific and choose two or three main keywords or phrases, then create an additional list of supporting keywords which you would like to be targeted (to a lesser degree) throughout the content on your website.
- Create a basic Website Design Plan of Action.

☑ **Purchase a Domain Name**

- If you have solidified your website plan, and you know your keywords - now you can purchase a domain name (if you haven't already). If possible, have the domain name containing the keywords that are being targeted.
- Not having your keywords in your domain name does not mean you won't gain a high search engine placement.

- I purchase from http://honestholly.com/goto/dynadot 📌 but you may want to wait until you sign-up for web hosting. Oftentimes, web hosting companies also sell domains. It may be easier to manage both domains and hosting in one central location.

☑ Web Hosting

Deciding which website hosting company to use is entirely up to you. My preferred website hosting company is Bluehost. If you purchase a 1-year plan with BlueHost, you will get a free domain name with the purchase.

Bluehost
Website: http://honestholly.com/goto/bluehosthr. 📌

☑ Add Keyword-Rich Articles
- Use your creativity to create a list of ideas for articles to be put on your website (containing the keywords you are targeting).
- Try to create 10-20 articles (or 10 to start, and add an article per week thereafter) which contain the keywords you are targeting, and support the overall theme.
- It's of paramount importance that you use the keywords you are targeting in the title of your article(s).
- Use many occurrences (tactfully, without being redundant) in the first two paragraphs especially, throughout the body and must also be in the closing paragraph. Each article should be 400-600 words in length.
- If you do not want to write the articles yourself, you can pay someone on Scriptlance to do the writing. Be specific about your keywords and instructions for the writer. (Cost per article is generally $5-10 dollars USD).
- Free articles may also be taken from an article directory website, which allows republishing (as long as the author bio or link is left intact). Try to keep this to a minimum, and have the majority of the content unique.

☑ **On-Site Search Engine Optimization**

- Go to Google Webmaster Tools at: http://honestholly.com/goto/webmasters ⚓ and sign-up for a free account. Login to the Google Sitemaps area and add your domain name.

- You may then go to: http://honestholly.com/goto/xmlsitemaps ⚓ to insert your URL and create a free sitemap. Save the sitemap file and follow the simple instructions on uploading it to your website. Finally, submit it to Google's Sitemaps so you can begin tracking your website details.

- The purpose of uploading your sitemap and submitting it to Google through the webmaster tools is to gain maximum exposure to all of the pages in your website by presenting them in an orderly fashion to the search engines.

- You will be able to track the Crawl Stats, Query Stats (popular keywords used to reach your website), Index Stats & Page Analysis. Integrate any and all Google Adsense ads and/or links to affiliate programs on your website.

The on-site SEO methods are extremely important (for your website to gain the highest ranking possible for whichever keywords you are targeting). Because of that, I want to be absolutely certain that you know how to complete each and every step – as I believe it is the key to your financial success.

The reason I state that is because the only way you will make an income from a website is to have it be of high quality, and have targeted groups of people being exposed to it. You need the traffic to create the wealth. I realize that some people are quite skilled in Google Adwords and other pay-per-click advertising methods. They do work – but for a small percentage of beginners. I always use the on-site SEO methods, and all of my niche sites have gained a top ranking – every one of them. It's difficult to know which program you might be creating a website in, but I have created several walk-through tutorials on completing all of the on-site optimization methods.

Reverse SEO Tip

If you are browsing your competitor's website and you want to see exactly what keywords were used for that particular page, open Internet Explorer. From there you can click on VIEW, then SOURCE, and you will be shown their title, keywords and description. Some pages are protected by webmasters who do not want people to see their keywords, in which case then nothing will appear. Alternatively they may have created a message for you, such as: "You're not supposed to be looking at my code." But, more often than not, you can view the code.

An Example of what may show up when you view the source:

```html
<html>

<head>

<meta http-equiv="Content-Type" content="text/html; charset=wind
<meta http-equiv="Content-Language" content="en-us">

<title>Tree Planting</title>
<meta name="keywords" content="planting trees,tree planting,how
<meta name="description" content="Tree Planting - Learn how to p
<meta name="GENERATOR" content="Microsoft FrontPage 4.0">
<meta name="ProgId" content="FrontPage.Editor.Document">

<meta name="Microsoft Border" content="none, default">
</head>
```

The code reveals the Title, Keywords and Description, which were inserted to help optimize the page. You can view source for each individual web page within a site.

CHAPTER 4: WEBSITE SEO ESSENTIALS

Google Webmaster Tools

Go to the Google Webmaster Tools website: http://honestholly.com/goto/webmasters 📌 and sign-up for a free account. Login to the Google Sitemaps area and add your domain name. It will allow you to manage numerous SEO-related tools for all of your websites, in one place. For each domain (or website) you add to your Google Webmaster account, you will be able to view important statistics, links, as well as optimize your sites further with several tools provided to you.

It's of extreme importance that you sign-up and use all of the tools that you can. Personally, I make most of my profits from Google's search engine traffic. If there is a way that Google has created a system to allow me to get more website exposure, I will use it. That's exactly what Google has created by making this great tool for users.

Site Maps

Site maps create a very specific path for the search engines and other crawlers to view all of the content that your website contains. This will create credibility for your website, while increasing its ranking by getting more pages indexed. Login to the Google site maps area and add your domain name.

You may then go to: http://honestholly.com/goto/xmlsitemaps 📌 to insert your URL and create a free sitemap. Save the sitemap file and follow the simple instructions on uploading it to your website. Finally, submit it to Google's site maps so you can begin tracking your website details.

Robots Text File

In order to allow or disallow the search engines to crawl and index your websites, you must create a special file and add it to your website. The file should be named: robots.txt and the purpose of the file is to tell the search engines to index the pages in your website. It basically gives the search engines permission to scan all the web pages on your website and list them in the search engines. The file is easy to create and you can make it in notepad.

☑ **Search Bots, Spiders, & Crawlers**

To create a clear path for your website to be indexed, the robots.txt basically tells the search engines about your website. Search engines have what is referred to as search bots, robots, spiders or crawlers – which are sent out to frequently view all websites on the Internet.

What a massive task these crawlers have, and it is an ongoing, nonstop process. So, to make the job more methodical and organized for the bots – web designers are encouraged to have a robots.txt file on each website. It should be uploaded to the root of the website. If your website is http://www.honestholly.com, then its location would be: http://www.honestholly.com/robots.txt.

Examples of the robots.txt file are below. For the website which you create to fully optimize to gain a top ranking in the search engines, you will want to add a robots.txt file that allows the spiders to index everything.

☑ **Allow All Spiders to Index Everything**

You can use the wildcard, * to let all spiders know they are welcome. The second, disallow, line you just leave empty.

User-agent: *
Disallow:

☑ **Disallow All Spiders from Indexing Your Site**

Warning: If you do this, your site will not gain a ranking in the search engines. Most people do not need to know how to do this, but some people have two sites with the same content. It is not advised to have duplicate content because Google and other search engines may ban both of your sites as a result.

This requires just a tiny change from the command above – be careful!

User-agent: *
Disallow: /

Statistics & Tracking

Statistics & tracking of website visitors is necessary to knowing what works, where your traffic is coming from, what they are clicking on and what they want to know more about.

There are several options available – one of the most popular is Google Analytics. It is free to open up a Google Analytics account. If you have already signed up a Google Account, then you can just login with your username here: http://honestholly.com/goto/analytics. ✈

Google Analytics provides precise, detailed information about your website visitors, where the people come from, how long he/she stays on a particular page, entry pages, exit pages, key words used to reach your website, referrals, etc. so you know exactly what advertising techniques are working for you and what you should improve on.

After logging into your free Google Analytics account area, you can add as many websites as you like. You then need to insert in a small piece of code into your website so the tracking can take place. Once this is done, the results are viewable online.

It shows the number of visits, page views, referring websites and keywords used to reach your website.

Heatmaps

Another method to monitor website statistical data is through the use of heatmaps. Heatmaps provide visual analysis of website visitor behavior, so you can truly optimize the performance of the website. An excellent provider of such a resource is CrazyEgg. Visit the website at: http://honestholly.com/goto/crazyegg ✈ for more information.

In addition to using heatmaps as a method to visually track and analyze your website visitors, CrazyEgg also has a full range of extensive tools to do even more tracking. You can learn about each and every element that is contained within your website. You will understand what visitors are interested in, what they are clicking on, how many clicks per link and the keywords they are using to reach your site, as well as the referrers.

CHAPTER 5: SEO TUTORIALS

Section 1: HTML SEO Tutorials

☑ Tutorial #1:

How to Add Custom Title, Description & Keywords to each page (Coffee Cup HTML Editor)

☑ Tutorial #2:

How to add alternate text to each and every image on your website (Coffee Cup HTML Editor)

Section 2: Wordpress SEO Tutorials

☑ Tutorial #1:

How to upload and Install the One Click plug-in through Bluehost's CPanel and your wordpress admin area.

Please Note: This tutorial is a visual step-by-step walkthrough for people who have wordpress installed, but want to add plug-ins (and aren't sure how to do so). This tutorial will teach you how to install "One Click" and it is the ONLY plug-in you will ever need to manually install ever again. After you install it, basically the plug-in transforms your normal wordpress admin area, so that you can (with only one click) install any plug-in or wordpress theme instantly (with no need to ever leave your admin area again). This means, you will never need to login to your bluehost account or CPanel area to manually upload plug-in or themes. If you sign-up for the free website service I offer, I already have "One Click" pre-installed for you – so you can skip this entirely.

☑ Tutorial #2:

How to add alternate text to each and every image on your website (Wordpress)

Section 1: Tutorial #1 – How to Add Custom Title, Description & Keywords

☑ First, open up Coffee Cup HTML Editor

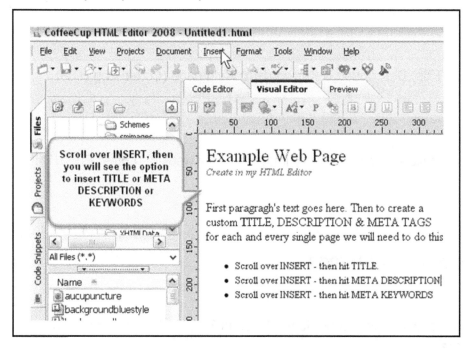

Open a specific page on your site (any page). Then, scroll over insert – a large dropdown box will appear.

☑ **Insert Title & Keywords**

Insert title, use your keywords and press ok when you are finished. Do the same for the description and meta tag keywords.

☑ **Overview**

The process of optimizing every single page of your website with your HTML editor is pretty straight-forward. It's just a matter of training yourself to do this each and every time you create a page. Always add the title, description and meta keywords. It will make a major difference in whether or not the search engines index your pages. The result – your site will either gain a high ranking for specific keywords you've targeted, or it will not.

☑ Alternate HTML Editors

If you are using an alternate HTML Editor (rather than using Coffee Cup HTML Editor) – the process is most likely similar to the one mentioned above. If you cannot find the option to insert the title, meta description and meta keywords, then open up the page you intend to work on.

Then anywhere in the area of the page, right click with your mouse. You should see a popup box that gives you some options – one should be "properties" or "page properties." Your best option would be to click on that, and try to insert the title, description and meta tags there. If all else fails, then try to find some tutorials online or a help index with the program you are using. This is so incredibly important, from an SEO standpoint, that you must know how to do it.

Section 1: Tutorial #2 – How to Add Alternate Text to Website Images

Adding alternate text to each image on your website is important for SEO, & also a standard for most webmasters. Many of my images have been indexed into Google's Image Search results due to the alternate text assigned to each.

Basically, CoffeeCup HTML Editor makes it pretty simple for you to add alternate text to an image (when you are actually inserting it). Click on "Insert Image," and you will see the screen below. Simply add the alternate text and save and exit.

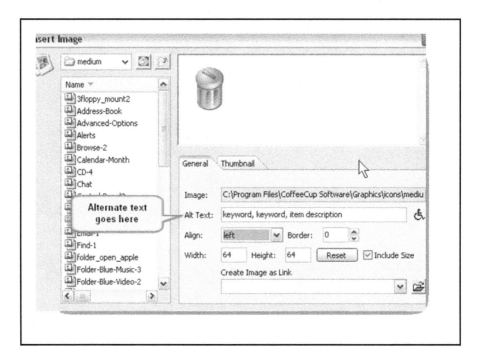

Adding Alternate Text to Images

Section 2: Tutorial #1 – How to Upload & Install One Click the Plug-in with Wordpress & Bluehost

☑ **Purpose of One Click**

The purpose of the "One Click" plug-in is to completely rid you of ever having to login to your hosting account to manually upload and install plug-ins again. This will be the last plug-in that you will ever need to install.

After installing "One Click," your wordpress admin area will be altered so you easily (with one click) add any wordpress plug-in or theme to your website (without ever leaving the admin area). It can be very difficult and time-consuming for people to upload plug-ins through your hosting account file management area. You will only need to do this process once, and the rest of your wordpress experiences should be smooth and easy. This tutorial is completely visual, to show you exactly how to upload the "One-Click" plug-in.

First, login to your webhosting account (Bluehost or an alternate hosting company).

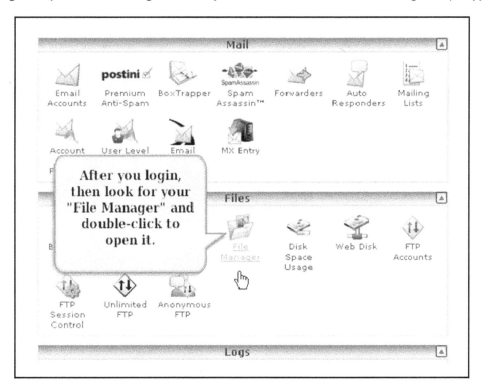

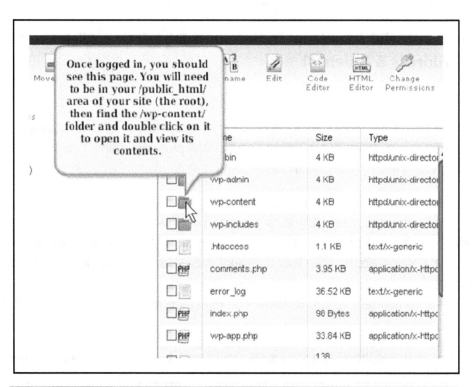

Once logged in, you should see this page. You will need to be in your /public_html/ area of your site (the root), then find the /wp-content/ folder and double click on it to open it and view its contents.

	Name	Size	Type
	bin	4 KB	httpd/unix-director
	wp-admin	4 KB	httpd/unix-director
	wp-content	4 KB	httpd/unix-director
	wp-includes	4 KB	httpd/unix-director
	.htaccess	1.1 KB	text/x-generic
	comments.php	3.95 KB	application/x-httpd
	error_log	36.52 KB	text/x-generic
	index.php	98 Bytes	application/x-httpd
	wp-app.php	33.84 KB	application/x-httpd

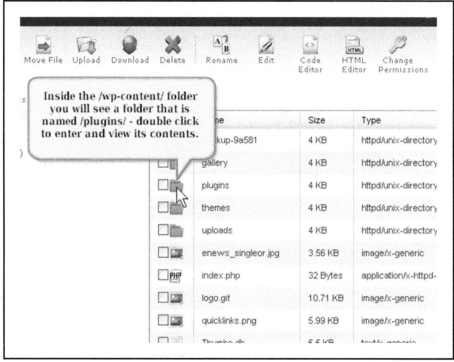

Move File	Upload	Download	Delete	Rename	Edit	Code Editor	HTML Editor	Change Permissions

Inside the /wp-content/ folder you will see a folder that is named /plugins/ - double click to enter and view its contents.

	Name	Size	Type
	kup-9a581	4 KB	httpd/unix-directory
	gallery	4 KB	httpd/unix-directory
	plugins	4 KB	httpd/unix-directory
	themes	4 KB	httpd/unix-directory
	uploads	4 KB	httpd/unix-directory
	enews_singleor.jpg	3.56 KB	image/x-generic
	index.php	32 Bytes	application/x-httpd-
	logo.gif	10.71 KB	image/x-generic
	quicklinks.png	5.99 KB	image/x-generic
	Thumbs.db	5.5 KB	text/x-generic

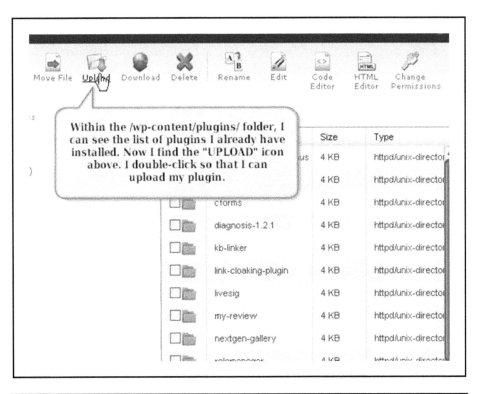

		Size	Type
	us	4 KB	httpd/unix-director
		4 KB	httpd/unix-director
☐ 📁	cforms	4 KB	httpd/unix-director
☐ 📁	diagnosis-1.2.1	4 KB	httpd/unix-director
☐ 📁	kb-linker	4 KB	httpd/unix-director
☐ 📁	link-cloaking-plugin	4 KB	httpd/unix-director
☐ 📁	livesig	4 KB	httpd/unix-director
☐ 📁	my-review	4 KB	httpd/unix-director
☐ 📁	nextgen-gallery	4 KB	httpd/unix-director
☐ 📁	rolomanager	4 KB	httpd/unix-director

Within the /wp-content/plugins/ folder, I can see the list of plugins I already have installed. Now I find the "UPLOAD" icon above. I double-click so that I can upload my plugin.

aximum File Size allowed for upload: 40.3 GB

ease select files to upload to **/home/buzztopi/public_html/kidwebguru/wp-conten**

Browse...
Browse...
Browse...

As soon as I double-clicked on that "UPLOAD" icon, this is the page I was brought to. Now I click on browse, to find the zip file (my plugin) on my computer to upload it to my website.

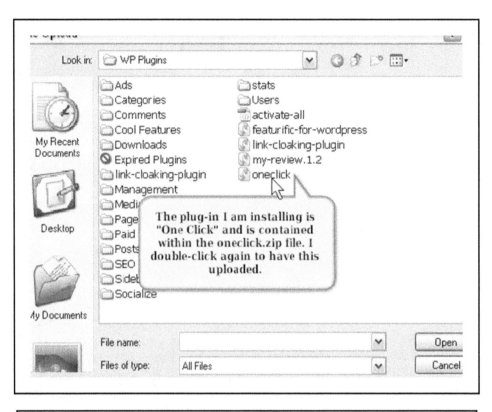

The plug-in I am installing is "One Click" and is contained within the oneclick.zip file. I double-click again to have this uploaded.

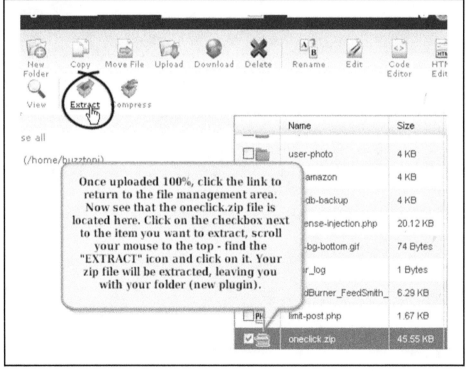

Once uploaded 100%, click the link to return to the file management area. Now see that the oneclick.zip file is located here. Click on the checkbox next to the item you want to extract, scroll your mouse to the top - find the "EXTRACT" icon and click on it. Your zip file will be extracted, leaving you with your folder (new plugin).

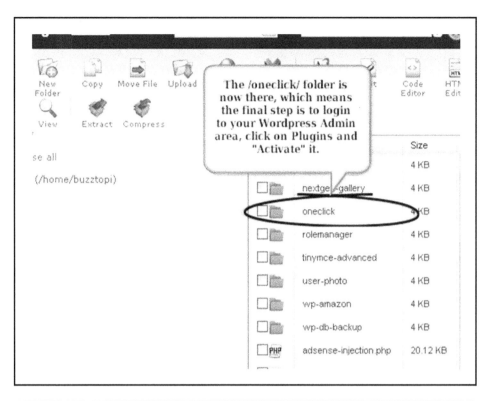

The /oneclick/ folder is now there, which means the final step is to login to your Wordpress Admin area, click on Plugins and "Activate" it.

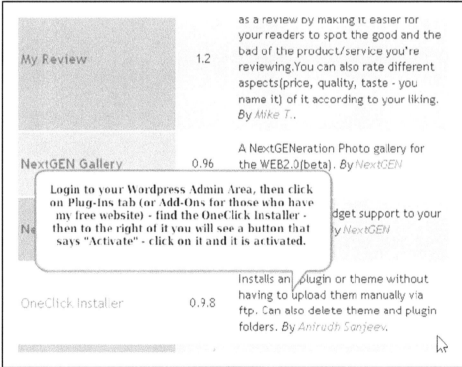

Login to your Wordpress Admin Area, then click on Plug-Ins tab (or Add-Ons for those who have my free website) - find the OneClick Installer - then to the right of it you will see a button that says "Activate" - click on it and it is activated.

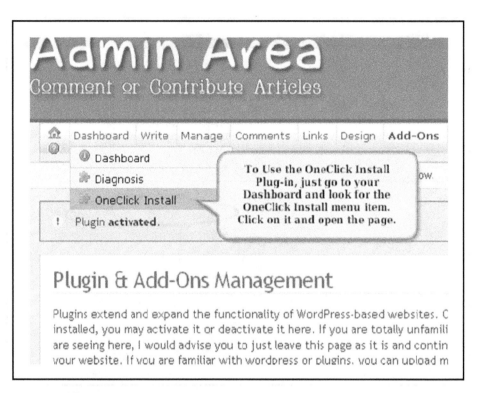

Admin Area
Comment or Contribute Articles

🏠 Dashboard Write Manage Comments Links Design **Add-Ons**

   ① Dashboard

   ✿ Diagnosis

   🔧 OneClick Install

!   Plugin **activated**.

> To Use the OneClick Install Plug-in, just go to your Dashboard and look for the OneClick Install menu item. Click on it and open the page.

Plugin & Add-Ons Management

Plugins extend and expand the functionality of WordPress-based websites. C installed, you may activate it or deactivate it here. If you are totally unfamili are seeing here, I would advise you to just leave this page as it is and contin your website. If you are familiar with wordpress or plugins, you can upload m

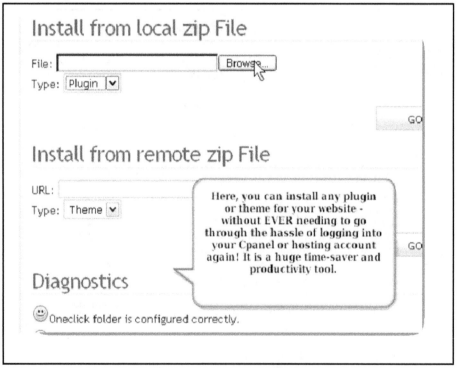

Install from local zip File

File: [   ] [Browse...]
Type: [Plugin ▼]

                                          GO

Install from remote zip File

URL: [   ]
Type: [Theme ▼]

> Here, you can install any plugin or theme for your website - without EVER needing to go through the hassle of logging into your Cpanel or hosting account again! It is a huge time-saver and productivity tool.

                                          GO

Diagnostics

☺ Oneclick folder is configured correctly.

Tutorial #2: How to Use the All-In-One SEO Plug-in with Wordpress to Optimize Each Page or Post

☑ **Requirements**

First, you must be using the self-hosted version of Wordpress (not a free Wordpress blog). Login to your Wordpress admin area.

In the All-In-One SEO settings page, be sure to use the keywords you are targeting. This page is vital to your SEO efforts & success. In addition to the options in the screenshot on the next page, you will also have the option to specify if you want a specific word (or words) to appear after the posts or pages you create.

For example, let's pretend I write a post one day about flowers in May. The title of the post is "Flowers in May" and the search engines will pick it up as the title of the particular web page, "Flowers in May." But if I specify that I want additional keywords or phrases to appear after the post or page title, it would help my SEO efforts significantly. If the key phrase I am targeting is "gardening guide," – then I would put that in my settings for the All-In-One SEO plug-in. So, the search engines would recognize the "Flowers in May" post, as having this title: Flowers in May – Gardening Guide. The title of all of my posts or all of my pages could contain a (short) list of my keywords or phrases.

In this screenshot, you can see the SEO Settings for my homepage. I specified the home page title, description and keywords. Below those options it also allows me to specify the page and post titles; as previously mentioned. On this screenshot it is not visible but you can view it in your settings.

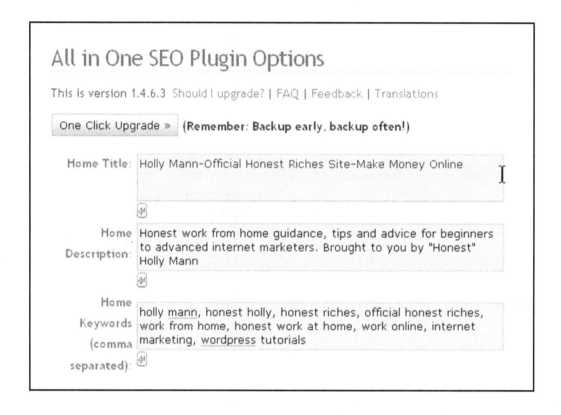

Book 6

Advertising

CHAPTER 1: PRESS RELEASE SUBMISSIONS

Power of Press Releases

Let's say you just finished designing and optimizing your website. You did everything you could do and now you must wait, as you submit articles and hope your website gains a high place in the search engines. It generally takes my websites 2-6 weeks to be indexed and about 8 weeks to have the high ranking for specific key phrases I optimize for (That is for websites I submit which have less than 1 million competing websites.)

When there is a large amount of competition it will take more time and effort to gain a high ranking. So, in the meantime you should get some highly targeted website traffic. If you want REAL traffic REAL fast (within 48 hours) then submit a press release. Submitting a press release to announce a website or a business development can drive a huge amount of targeted visitors to your website. Press releases are designed to announce business-related events and should be news-worthy.

For example, someone releasing a new e-book or software program can create a press release to gain more exposure. Use your imagination – I try to write a quick press release for every single website I create and oftentimes the release is thrown together. It's ok to do that, but keep it simple, written as well as possible, and news-worthy. Feel free to copy anything from a release I submitted for Free with PRWeb.com. PRWeb.com is no longer offering free submissions – so I have included a list of Press Release Submission sites which are free, on page 143.

Press Release Example

Cheap Inexpensive Web Hosting Services List & Comparisons

Finding an affordable web hosting service for your personal, business or ecommerce website can be overwhelming if you are new to the Internet website hosting world.

Web hosting services all range in features and price, so it is important to have a wide variety of website hosting options before making a purchase. One must consider the size of space needed on the website hosting server, the amount of allotted bandwidth, whether to have Windows hosting, Linux hosting or a dedicated or virtual hosting server. It may be overwhelming and sound quite complicated, that is why a professional website designer has created a list of her personal favorite hosting companies. The list also includes information about every type of website hosting plan, from business web hosting, cgi web hosting, dedicated web hosting, asp web hosting, ecommerce web hosting and the cheapest web hosts. It also includes a "Blacklist of Hosting Companies," and that details some customers' negative experiences with particular web hosting companies. The information can help the public in choosing the best hosting plan.

The website reports, comparisons and recommendations are online and viewable to the public at: http://honestholly.com/goto/ehosting.

(Please note: this website is no longer being updated or maintained, and is only used as an example)

Actual PRWeb Statistics:

Statistic	Count	Description
Reads	3,296	This number tells you how many times it was read.
Estimated Pickup	45	This number estimates the number of times your press release was picked up by a media outlet.
Prints	2	Number of times that someone has printed your press release.

Even if you are just announcing a new website and would like to draw in some traffic before it is indexed by the search engines, creating a press release is an excellent option. It can create a huge amount of buzz about your website. I normally only have time to create one press release per site. Press release companies team up with leading news sources and agents to help people share newsworthy events. By submitting a press release, partner websites and search engines will display the releases.

Exposure=Traffic=Sales.

Free Press Release Websites List

I-Newswire
Website: http://honestholly.com/goto/inews

PRLog
Website: http://honestholly.com/goto/prlog

Free-Press-Release
Website: http://honestholly.com/goto/freepr

PRFree
Website: http://honestholly.com/goto/prfreesite

24-7 Press Release
Website: http://honestholly.com/goto/24pr

PR.com
Website: http://honestholly.com/goto/pr

Press Release Point
Website: http://honestholly.com/goto/presspoint

Paying for Extra Exposure

These services are all free. If you wish to pay for extra exposure, search engine optimization, listings and inclusion - the many of the websites listed above provide you with the option to do that as well. I normally donate $10 through PayPal and that increases the exposure and traffic. PRWeb.com offers paid placement options and assistance to gain exposure for your press release in all the major search engines.

☑ **Press Release Tip**

PR.com, http://honestholly.com/goto/pr press releases are often indexed by Google's News Section. This greatly increases the exposure it receives, thus returning you with a lot of targeted traffic. Numerous other free press release distribution websites may do the same; it's just a matter of sending it in, and testing the services.

Press Releases Must Be In this Format

FOR IMMEDIATE RELEASE: Type these words in the upper left-hand margin, just under your letterhead. Be sure to capitalize every letter.

Contact Information: Skip two lines after release statement and list the name, title, and telephone and fax numbers of your company contact person.

Headline: Skip two lines after your contact information and bold your headline text.

Dateline: This should be the city your press release is issued from and the date you are mailing your release.

Lead Paragraph: The first paragraph should be a "hook." It needs to grab your reader's attention, as well as containing the important information to your message. Make sure you include the five W's (who, what, when, where and why).

Text: Body of the press release in which you give full details about the event.

Recap: At the lower left hand corner of your last page, re-state your product's specifications, highlight a product release date.

CHAPTER 2: ARTICLES & DIRECTORIES

Spreading the Word

Spreading the word about your website, to gain traffic, links and ranking, takes only a few simple methods. First, I recommend that you write several articles which contain useful information related to your website. Then, submit those articles to several online article website. This not only drives targeted traffic to your website, but creates a name for you as an expert in your field. The best site to start with is Ezine Articles.

Ezine Articles

Website: http://honestholly.com/goto/ezinearticles ✎

It also has a viral affect because once you submit your article; other related website owners can reprint it on their website (only under the condition that they keep your author bio intact). Your author bio area should contain a summary of who you are and/or what your website is about – and link to it. This is a powerful way to create a lot of links to your website. It drives traffic while increasing your exposure and reach online.

To search for articles that allow reprinting, or to find article directory websites (so you can post your content) visit: Articles Hub at: http://honestholly.com/goto/articleshub. ✎

There are thousands of article submission websites online, which allow you to publish your work and have others reprint it as well. The websites are constantly changing, so I prefer not to put a huge list of them in this book (as I do not want to provide you with a bunch of broken links).

> **Useful Tip:**
> When you are doing research on your niche or keywords you want to target, take note of the website and articles that show up for those keywords. Try to keep track of any article websites that show up. This is important because you can then see which article sites have a tendency of getting picked-up and indexed by the search engines. If you submit an article, be sure to use the keywords you are targeting in the title. It may be the deciding factor in whether or not your article is listed higher in the search engines.

Directory Submissions

A website directory is a website which includes listings of other websites on the web; according to topic or a category that your website falls under. If your website is included in online directories which hold relevance in the search engines that can help boost your ranking. You can use the list of online directories that your main competing websites submitted to, as well as submitting your site to some of the following directories listed below. It is important that the sites you submit to are relevant sites, hold no "red flags" and are not spam sites.

To be safe, you can check that they are before submitting your website to them through: http://honestholly.com/goto/siteadvisor.

List of Directories

ABC Submission
Website: http://honestholly.com/goto/abcsubmission

Suggest Link
Website: http://honestholly.com/goto/suggestlink

Sites Directory
Website: http://honestholly.com/goto/sitesdirectorynet

Classified Ads

Creating short, attention-grabbing ads and posting them to free online classifieds can create an income stream. You can link the ads to your personal blog or website – or directly to your affiliate website that you are promoting. Be sure to read the Terms of Service and usage before you post so that you do not violate the rules and/or get banned from posting.

Knowing your niche – and the people who you are trying to reach is very important. Post in a specific category that relates to the topic at hand. If possible, use keywords in the title of your post.

Craigslist
Website: http://honestholly.com/goto/craigslist ✒

- Hugely popular totally free online classifieds system
- Searchable by city, state, country (huge database of listings)
- Ads are commonly indexed with high ranking in the search engines
- You are not allowed to place duplicate ads in differing cities and doing so will cause the site to ban your IP address and ban you from posting

USFreeads
Website: http://honestholly.com/goto/usfreeads ✒

- Ads are commonly indexed with high ranking in the search engines
- Free to post classified ads
- Advanced tracking to view hits, visitors and those who have read the ad
- You are allowed to post duplicate ads in differing categories

Topix Classifieds
Website: http://honestholly.com/goto/topixclassifieds ✒

- Ads are commonly indexed with high ranking in the search engines if keywords are used in the title and ad (and there isn't a huge amount of competition)
- Terms of service for use and placing ads is available here: http://honestholly.com/goto/topixterms ✒

CHAPTER 3: ESTABLISHING YOUR PRESENCE

Become an Expert in Your Field

Establishing your expertise online is another method to driving targeted, repeat visitors to your website. You are representing not only yourself, but the product or service which you are promoting. There is an increase in the number of websites which allow users to be "go-to" experts, and share knowledge while gaining credibility.

If you have a website, you will need to learn about whatever it is you are promoting or creating your website about. You will need to either pay someone to write for you, or you will need to write articles about your website theme. You can use the work you have already written, and submit it online.

How-To Websites

eHow

Website: http://honestholly.com/goto/ehow 📌

The classic "how-to" website is eHow. The website allows regular users to sign-up and contribute "how-to" articles. It's more than simple to do this, and does not require extensive writing. After you join and you know what you want to write your "how-to" article about, then you begin the process of completing a small series of "fill-in-the-blanks" to complete the article.

Once it is done, you will see a link that goes to the author's page (for whoever wrote that particular article). This can create credibility for you as an author. You can also place a link back to your website on the author page, as well as a personal summary. This will drive targeted traffic to your main website(s).

If your website is not yet indexed by Google or other major search engines, this will also make that happen a lot quicker. Websites like this one tend to have a high ranking and a high number of pages indexed in the search engines. Sometimes within hours of creating a post, Google spiders will crawl and index it.

If the spiders are crawling and indexing your post, and the author bio section is linking to your website, then your site will be crawled (and most likely indexed) as well. The individual article how-to pages usually get indexed fast.

Other readers can comment on your articles, and the website is quite social and interactive. When you don't know how to do something, where do you go for advice when friends or family don't have a clue? The Internet. Most searches with the words "how-to" blank will result in pulling up one of the many how-to articles from this website.

WikiHow

Website: http://honestholly.com/goto/wikihow 📌

This is another popular "how-to" website that has been created by users for users. Just join, and begin your "how-to" writing. My recommendation is to create your author profile as soon as possible. While conducting research, I noticed that the wikiHow website also shows the number of times each page has been viewed (at the bottom of the page).

Many pages have been viewed more than 20,000 times, shortly after the article was posted. Can you imagine the possibilities if you write about your niche and reach all those targeted visitors? If it is well-written and useful to the reader, he or she will most likely check out your website for more information.

WonderHowTo

Website: http://honestholly.com/goto/wonderhowto 📌

A highly interactive website which allows users to contribute "how-to" videos, for every topic imaginable. This popular, interactive website could literally drive tens of thousands (or more) visitors back to your main website. If you provide quality, useful content, or entertaining videos then the users will come back for more. You can create "how-to" videos with any cell phone camera (that allows video recording), digital camera or camcorder. Each video has a link to the creator's website (if he/she has one), as well as options for viewers to grade the videos (A,B,C,D,F).

Consistency & Quality

Whether you are creating content to share on your website, or on article directory websites or "how-to" sites, the key to creating a following is consistency and quality. You need to be knowledgeable in all aspects of your niche or topic that you are writing about. You need to attempt to find information that is useful and of high quality, that might really help the reader in some way. Anything that answers a reader's questions, concerns or provides them a way to save time or help them with something – is generally thought of as useful.

Don't create posts or articles for the sole purpose of promoting products and trying to make money on affiliate sales. Doing that occasionally is ok, but the customer or reader should always be top priority. Providing them with information or a service that will benefit them, will also benefit you in the long run. Writing well and writing often is imperative. Not everyone is good at updating their website and creating fresh new content, but try your best to do so.

Create a Free Report

If your niche website is already online and receiving a little traffic, you may want to consider creating a free report to give away. Why would you do that, you wonder? Well, many expert marketers would agree that the sales process has many steps, and that you should not worry about the frontend product (but the backend sales).

Does that sound like Greek? Well, I will provide more details.

Let's go back to the idea I mentioned earlier, the example website I created for parents of multiples. Let's say, I have created a lot of specialized content, targeted to reach my niche market. I am receiving traffic to the website, but only making a small profit on ads that are resulting in sales. I feel frustrated, but do not give up. I create a totally free downloadable report to give away to website visitors. Sounds simple enough, right?

It is simpler than you know, because once setup and put into place – you could be making more money than you ever imagined. If you are wondering how that is possible, with a free report, continue reading to learn how. First, the website visitors are at your site seeking information to help them save money and gather information from others who are parents of multiples. They visit your site, like what they are reading and you have quality information and articles.

You have created your free report to let website visitors know all of your tried and true techniques to getting a huge assortment of baby products, diapers and formula for free. The report does not need to be too long, but it must have details and solid information. (Please note: In Book 7, Chapter 1, I teach you how to create e-books and distribute them online).

☑ Subscriber Opt-In Box

The website visitor is impressed with what you have to offer, and clicks on the link that you have placed on your site that says, "Click here to get the free report." Once the person clicks on the link, he/she will be taken to the next page.

The next page will contain a subscribe box which says, please fill in your first name and e-mail address and the report will be e-mailed to you immediately. Or, you can have the person redirected to the download page. It's also a good idea to put a clearly stated disclaimer, so the people know that you will not spam, sell or give out their private e-mail addresses. Now, the next step involves either an up sell directly after the user hits enter and you receive his or her e-mail address, or else you can save the up sell for inside the free report.

☑ Up sells

What is an up sell? Well, a classic example of an up sell that you might encounter in everyday life is when you are at a fast food restaurant. You order a meal, and the cashier asks if you would like to upsize the fries for "x" amount of money.

It's generally a method to sell you something after you've already made a small purchase, so that you already have money in hand and are more willing to buy something else. It's a proven method that is used throughout the world. Psychologically, what makes the person more willing to buy after either downloading the free report, or after making a small purchase? Well, first I want to clarify that I don't endorse deceiving or manipulating people to try to earn extra money. This technique here is one which is truly important to share, because the income potential with it is huge.

But, please be cautious in the way you create the offer or deal, because your customer should be your top priority. Whatever you are trying to sell with your one-time offer or backend product should completely over-deliver and be offered at an extremely reasonable price. Some people have felt compelled to buy a product (or a whole package of products) in a one-time-offer because there is just so much offered, and the price is right.

I've seen dozens of one-time offers in my online ventures, and I can honestly attest that I have almost always purchased the $10 packages. The average price point that one-time offer creators set varies, from $10, $17, $27, $47, $97 and so on. The price can be set by you, and you can also do testing to see what you have the highest rate of conversion with. It's odd, but sometimes a higher price means you will have more sales. Sometimes when you offer a product of such high value, then set the price a little higher, the perceived value increases instantly.

"Perceived value" of an item or product you sell is based on numerous factors, and viewed differently from person to person.

Before explaining that further, I just want to reiterate the importance of customer satisfaction. Making changes to increase the perceived value of your product is a positive route to take, but only if what you are offering is truly of high value and worth.

If everything looks extremely well-done and then the customer realizes you have created this amazing sales page and the product does not meet the standards you set, the customer will be upset, lose all trust and ask for a refund. That person may in return, tell others to avoid you or your websites.

That is what you absolutely do not want to happen. It only takes a single person to greatly damage the reputation of another Internet Marketer. It also only takes one person to create credibility, trust and loyalty by sharing their good experiences and dealings with you. Keep that in mind.

A product of high value should be well-packaged, cleanly put together and offer complete clarity in the sales page. No doubt should arise in the potential customer's mind. There are minor changes a webmaster can make when creating an item to sell, or packing the item to put on a one-time offer page.

☑ Increasing Perceived Value

Simple adjustments to the layout, terms and other elements on your sales page will greatly increase customer satisfaction and perceived value. In return, more customers will be satisfied, and proud to promote your services or products to others. If you under-deliver in any aspect of the process, you will not only be doing a disservice to yourself, but to others as well. Word-of-mouth advertising, one which spreads freely from one happy customer to another is extremely powerful.

Keep the sales page clean, simple and to-the-point. Focus on the benefits of the product or service, rather than just describing it.

Do not over-hype or exaggerate – be as honest as possible. This is one thing that I have seen repeatedly, especially on one-time-offer pages. People make promises to you that you could make $1000 dollars or even $10,000 dollars with very little effort or work. Do not go overboard in your wording.

If you in fact are not making the same $1000 or $10,000 dollars per day with very little effort, absolutely do not tell others they can do that. Lying and leading others down the wrong path will create instant distrust in your name and brand.

Refund policies increase trust in the potential buyers, and should be clearly stated underneath the "buy now" button or elsewhere on the page.

It should be visible and with no hidden terms – very straight-forward. It also helps to put a seal or certificate image that says "Satisfaction Guaranteed or Money Back." Testimonials add a great deal of credibility to a seller instantly. Brief, honest testimonials from people who have purchased will help.

You could put a couple of them on the homepage and add a link to "View More Testimonials." If you have any trouble gathering testimonials after you first create the website or sales page, then you can offer your product for free to a select few. All you ask in return is an honest evaluation or testimonial if they are satisfied.

Photos help add to the sales page and seller's credibility immensely. People say a picture can tell a thousand words. If you feel comfortable, adding a picture with a personalized note from you will help a lot. With so many sellers online and so many websites with similar looking sales pages (especially with one-time offers) – adding a little personal touch helps a lot. If concerned about your appearance, I would say to try not to be. People all look different and sometimes that is what can make you stand apart and draw more people into you.

The main thing to keep in mind when adding a photo of yourself or testimonial photos is to make sure the photo is of decent quality; not blurry or dark. Add a contact me link, so visitors can e-mail you with questions. Do not put your e-mail address on any webpage anywhere. People often wonder why their inbox with yahoo mail or another mail service is totally full of spam – that is why. If you put your e-mail address online, unfortunately it can too easily be taken and used against you (by automated software that is trying to take e-mail addresses to spam you).

If you absolutely feel inclined to give your personal e-mail, be sure to type it in a format that would not be crawlable by the automated e-mail stealers. For example: mye-mailaddress (at) gmail.com is the appropriate way to give out this e-mail address: mye-mailaddress@gmail.com. Frequently asked questions also add clarity to any sales page. In addition, you will receive fewer e-mails from confused or unsure potential customers. Clean, crisp design and modern graphics used sparingly on your sales page can increase perceived value greatly.

Tutorial: Free Report & Time-Sensitive Offer Process

This tutorial will explain, in depth all that you need to create a free report and a time-sensitive offer (also known as "one time offer"). Some of the details below are technical, but all are explained thoroughly.

☑ Creating the Free Report

The first step in this process is for you to create your free report. To create a high quality, professional-looking report, it is recommended that you type your report with decent word-processing software (rather than WordPad or a simple text editor).

Many computers have Microsoft Word or some type of alternative.

If you do not have Microsoft Word, then I recommend that you download Open Office at: http://honestholly.com/goto/openoffice.

It is a free "productivity suite" that is easy-to-use and offers word-processing capabilities, plus an array of other uses (spreadsheet creation, databases, presentations) that might be needed for other projects.

☑ Revising and Finalizing

It's important that you revise, edit and finalize your product. Use spell-check and also (if possible) ask a friend or relative to carefully read over your report, point out any inconsistencies or grammatical problems. Try to be aware of your writing weaknesses – so you can more easily spot them and correct the errors. Another method is to read your words out loud, and if they sound a little awkward or out of place – revise and rewrite.

☑ Converting to a PDF File

A PDF File (Portable Document Format) is a commonly used file format for reports, e-books and newsletters.

The reason it is so commonly used and recommended is because the creator of the document intends to format the document in a way that all viewers will see the same thing.

If your report is created in Microsoft Word, or in Open Office Software, the person who sees or receives the file could have a different version of the software and the file might look distorted or not show up correctly.

Different browsers, computer screen sizes, resolution and software can all be contributing factors and problems.

So, to avoid it all – it is recommended that you convert your Word Document (or Open Office document) from its original format into a PDF format. PDF Files make it easier to keep the style, fonts and formatting intact so that viewers can see and print it without any problems.

Professional PDF Creation Software

Adobe Acrobat
Website: http://honestholly.com/goto/acrobat 📌

Create Adobe@PDF Online
Website: http://honestholly.com/goto/adobefree 📌

PDF Forge
Website: http://honestholly.com/goto/pdfforge 📌

☑ **Creating the Time Sensitive Offer WebPages**

The methods used to actually create the time sensitive offer pages, vary depending on what type of website you have (whether you are using html, php, wordpress or an alternate web creator).

Either way, you will need to create an "opt-in" page for the people to subscribe to download the product. Next, you will need to create the page that the subscriber is redirected to. This page will either be a "thank you" page with instructions to download their free product, or the time-sensitive offer page.

Because there are so many web design options, it is difficult to advise specific methods to create the web pages for the time-sensitive offers.

So, I will focus on one specific method to create your time-sensitive offer page. If it is not in your range of expertise or you feel there is an alternative option that would better suit you, then feel free to try that. Hiring a freelancer (for those who are not technically inclined) is also an excellent option, and highly affordable.

☑ **Free PHP One-Time-Offer Script**

An excellent free one-time-offer script, created by David John Thomas, can be downloaded here: http://honestholly.com/goto/freeotoscript. 📌

The script can be downloaded at the website, and then installed on your hosting server. Once the script is in place and you have your pages created, you're ready to add the payment buttons.

☑ The Item(s) to Offer

This part of the process is an important one. First, it is recommended that you offer only products which relate to the topic at hand. If the website is about taking care of triplets, then the time-sensitive offer should include items related to parenting, multiples, managing a home, babies, etc. I recommend that you do a search online and purchase the Master Resale Rights to a product or array of products related to your website. Master Resale Rights (MRR) products are ones which you can purchase and resell while keeping 100% of the profits as your own. Please read Book 9: Chapter 4, for complete instructions on how to profit with MRR products, where and how to purchase them.

☑ Payment Buttons & Redirect

On the actual time-sensitive offer page, below the offer description you will need to put a "buy now" button or payment button of some sort. Your choice of payment processors to use is entirely up to you. If you have no experience selling online, I would recommend that you use PayPal, Clickbank or Plimus to start with. All are simple to use, and to create payment buttons that allow redirects (to the download pages).

☑ Download Page

After the user purchases the time-sensitive offer, he will be redirected to the product download page. If the payment processor you use is PayPal, you can specify the redirect page. This means, you will need to manually create another page that will say "Thank you for purchasing."

It should also say something in regards to the fact that the payment has been processed and a receipt will be e-mailed. And, it will contain direct download links to the products that were purchased.

If you manually create the download page and put it on the same website you are selling on, it's important to protect it.

Put the download page and the files in separate parts of your website. If your website is: http://www.website.com, then try to put your download page deep into folders and subfolders (so people do not easily locate or swipe your files).

Example of a download page: http://www.website.com/n23/jntre/r45/files.

If using Plimus as a payment processor, your files will be securely located on their server. So, after the user makes his purchase and it clears, then he will be sent a receipt by e-mail (automatically) as well as a secure download of his product through Plimus.

It makes it impossible for website visitors to steal your products, because they will be securely held on the Plimus server.

CHAPTER 4: PAY-PER-CLICK ADVERTISING

Google Adwords

If you do not want to wait for a higher placement through free advertising, you can try Google AdWords or Yahoo Overture. The programs charge you Pay-Per-Click (PPC) or per site visitor. This basically means that you will be paying for your website visitors.

You can create short ads and each time someone views (and clicks on) your ad, you are charged a certain amount of money.

Google Adwords is a method of advertising which displays an ad (which you create, including a title and a couple of sentences) that will show up on the Google Search engine along the right-hand side of the page. If you take a look at Google you will see the Sponsored ads on the right side and those are the PPC Ads.

With Google AdWords you create your own ads, choose keywords to help match your ads to your audience and pay only when someone clicks on them. The ads will show up on the right-hand column of the search results page. Cost per-click varies depending on the ad placement, topic and amount of competition. Rest assured, you are allowed to set a maximum amount per day and per month – that way you do not go over-budget and spend all of your money.

Please understand that Google PPC advertising is a risky venture to become involved with. It's a risky venture that can offer high returns if you play your cards right and promote the correct product.

If you find something that is a "niche," without many competing ads (so the cost for your ads is low) then you can make a decent amount of money. The hard part, in which many people give up on the whole PPC concept – is in the trial and error.

It is costly and I don't recommend this unless you have a little extra money to put into testing and creating a proper campaign.

Creating Your PPC Campaign

The first piece of advice is for you to create the framework needed to run a pay-per-click campaign. Although it is possible to throw a few ads out there and hope for the best, it is not recommended.

The first step is to conduct thorough keyword research. The same research you would have needed to do if you were to optimize your website. Thorough keyword research techniques are explained here in Book 2, Chapter 3.

After you have conducted the keyword research, you should have a substantial list of keywords and key phrases.

If you were just optimizing your website, I would recommend that you have a few main keywords or key phrases, and a handful of supporting ones as well. If you are creating a PPC campaign, it is ok to increase your list of keywords and key phrases. This is important for testing purposes – so you can have more options when you learn which key phrases are most profitable and ones which are not. By weeding out the non-profitable key phrases, you will save yourself a lot of campaign costs.

☑ **Grouping the Keywords**

After you have a substantial list of keywords and key phrases related to your website and products, then it is a good idea to group them with similar key phrases. This is for organizational and testing purposes. It is also important because you can customize your landing page so that certain keywords or key phrases, will lead the visitor to a specific page related to that.

☑ **Landing Pages**

A landing page is the actual webpage that the specific PPC campaign will link to. For example, let's say I am using Google Adwords PPC Advertising for my "parents of multiples" website. I have decided to group similar keywords together.

This landing page is one which I specifically created for my Group 1 Keywords and campaign.

I did not direct the visitors to the homepage, rather specifically to a page which directly relates to the keywords they typed into Google.

This creates an instant appeal to them because it is exactly what they were seeking. They weren't seeking to reach your homepage and browse around – they specifically looked for "cheap multiples clothing," and the page they are brought to is only about that.

```
Group 1 Keywords:

"clothing for multiples"
"clothing for twins"
"clothing multiples"
"cheap multiples clothing"

Group 1 Landing Page:
http://www.websitename.com/cheapmultiplesclothing.htm

Group 2 Keywords:

"multiples support groups"
"advice parents multiples"
"advice parents twins"
"guide parents multiples"

Group 2 Landing Page:
http://www.websitename.com/multiplesparentsguide.htm
```

The Group 2 landing page was created specifically for people who were seeking a guide or resources and articles to help support parents of multiples.

If someone was seeking this, he would be in need of some solid information, and he'd probably be ready to pay for it. If you have a product to sell, which relates to caring for multiples or children in general, you could promote it on this page. If you do not, you can promote Amazon.com books which are related to this very topic, and earn commissions on all sales resulting.

☑ Testing Campaigns

After organizing all of your ad groups and separate campaigns, now split testing can begin. Split-testing is when you create two different ads for the same campaign. You can leave the headlines the same (for consistency) and change the actual short description or ad text. Google Adwords will monitor all clicks and tell you how many each ad receives. I recommend you test them for a few days (or longer, depending on your budget) and get rid of the one that is receiving less quality traffic, clicks and sales. An example of split-testing, for the first example campaign created for "cheap clothing for multiples" is this:

Two ads were created for one specific campaign, related to "cheap multiples clothing." The headlines were the same, and the ad text varied slightly. After running this campaign for a couple of days, I will get rid of the one with the least amount of quality clicks and conversions. It's a simple method to save you money in advertising costs, and increase the quality, highly targeted traffic.

☑ **Attention-Grabbing Ads**

Creating ads that grab attention will get you more clicks. If you have a website about "The Best and Worst Web Hosting Companies Online", have your ad say something like "BLACKLIST of hosting companies to avoid" so that more people will click on your ad and visit your site than the other, normal web hosting review sites posted.

☑ **Attention-Grabbing Words**

Blacklist	Rare
Essential	Revealed
Hot News	Secrets
Instant	Special
Odd	Strange
Quality	Unique

CHAPTER 5: AFFORDABLE ADVERTISING

Adbrite Advertising

Once your website is up and running and you are working on optimizing it but want more traffic than what you are getting from forums and blogs, then it's time to do some smart advertising.

Adbrite is a marketplace for buyers and sellers of website ad space. If you're an advertiser, you can search or browse to find a site you want to advertise on. Then you can view relevant stats, including price and how many clicks you can expect. It's really simple and fast: to order, you add it to your cart, write your ad, and pay. If approved by the webmaster, your ad will appear on that site at the scheduled time (usually within 24 hours).

Adbrite

Website: http://honestholly.com/goto/adbrite

If you're a publisher, use AdBrite to set your own ad rates, and approve or reject every ad that's purchased for your site.

AdBrite enables you to instantly sell ads to your visitors via a "Your Ad Here" link, in addition to selling through AdBrite's marketplace and sales team. Selling ad space is a good way to make some extra money - the more traffic equals the higher price you can make the ad space for sale or rent.

On the following page you can view a screenshot from AdBrite for one of the thousands of sites you can choose to advertise on.

Adbrite Example Ad

As you can see, it costs $15.00 to advertise on that site for one week. It receives over 790,000 page views per day - and that is a lot of traffic. If you have a website or product you would like to promote that goes hand-in-hand with online gaming then that's a good price for advertising.

AZoogleAds

AZoogleAds is an ad-network connecting publishers with advertisers. If you are a publisher, meaning if you have a website, you can earn revenue by placing ads on your website.

If you are seeking targeted traffic, you can create ads that will drive traffic back to your website. If you are seeking to get targeted traffic, then AZoogleAds is an option that will deliver targeted traffic right to your website. You can create an online ad campaign in minutes.

AZoogleAds
Website: Website: http://honestholly.com/goto/azoogle

AZoogleAds has created a tool called "Epic Ad Center," which comprises of several wizards and programs that help you create the actual ads for your campaign.

Not everyone is familiar with editing images and creating graphics, so this will make that process a breeze. You can use one of the wizards to create professional display ads, coupon ads or text ads. You can either upload your own ads (based on images, graphics or videos) or you can use the AZoogleAds wizard to create ads on the site.

WidgetBucks

WidgetBucks is an ad network that is increasing in growth and popularity online. The simple 3-step process is what is quite appealing to the non-technical types. You just sign-up, then customize your widget and get a piece of code, then put the code into your website to start earning. You will earn money each time someone clicks through the widget to the advertiser's site.

WidgetBucks

Website: Website: http://honestholly.com/goto/widgetbucks ✔

What is a widget? A widget is a piece of code that can be copied and pasted into your website. The piece of code can have many uses. For example, let's say I create a widget, which is a piece of code that will display a box and count-down timer.

I will use the "parents of multiples" website example again. Let's say that I have created a countdown timer widget that says: My Multiples are Due In…One Month and three days. That particular widget could be useful for anyone who is expecting to give birth to twins or multiples and has a website. If I am pregnant with triplets, and I have a website, I would most definitely want to use that neat widget to share with others my due date.

So, widgets all have different purposes. Generally, widgets can be interactive for users. For the countdown widget, the person who wants to use the widget would need to enter in some details about her due date. That widget will then output the specific correct approximate due date and any other related details. Underneath the widget, or contained within it, there should be a link to the creator's website that says: "Do you want this widget? Get it free here," or something similar. This is a viral marketing tactic.

The creator has made something very useful for expecting parents of multiples, so as others see it (and also want it) they can obtain the same code. Widgets end up virally spreading around your niche, as others with similar interests find it useful too.

Other widget examples are simple news aggregators. If I have my main website, http://www.honestholly.com but I would like to put all the recent posts from my forum on it, I can do so through a widget. The widget can take the latest posts and continually update my widget with it. This will save me time and energy so I do not need to manually input new items every day.

With WidgetBucks, you will be able to take a piece of widget code from the site, and then put it on your website. It will automatically take ads and put them on your widget (and update and change them regularly) depending on your website content. That way, you have content and niche-specific ads reaching your target market.

You will earn money each time someone clicks through the widget to the advertiser's site. Please refer to the earnings details and terms of service for updated information about that.

Book 7

Product Creation

CHAPTER 1: CREATING AN E-BOOK

It is no secret that people are searching the Internet day-in and day-out for more information.

What are people searching for? Answers, assistance, entertainment, healing, learning materials and products to help them achieve different kinds of success.

Believe it or not, many people have strong interests and expertise in a topic or subject, which others may relate to.

We're in the Internet Information age. The Internet is easy to access for most people, convenient and less work than picking up a paperback book.

There's no need to run off to a bookstore when you have all of the reading materials you want at your fingertips and can purchase one with the click of a mouse.

Due to the ease of purchasing online, regular people who have a desire to share their information, secrets, recipes, stories or helpful solutions can do so and become published online. Their published product can be sold as an E-Book or downloadable E-product. If you are passionate about a topic, you feel that you are experienced enough to write about it or have someone write an E-Book for you on the subject; you could start reaping the benefits of working online as a published E-book author.

The reason this is so lucrative compared to publishing a hard copy of a book is because you have no overhead costs, no printing fees, no shipping and handling or anything other than miniscule online payment processor fees.

The following tutorial will explain, in detailed, step-by-step format exactly how to conceptualize your e-book idea, plan it, research, write, promote it, create a website and sell it online.

Tutorial: Researching, Creating & Selling an E-Book Online

Step 1: Conduct Research

You must realize that although you may be an expert on the topic, there might be hundreds of others who have already written e-books on the exact subject.

You must be realistic, know your competition and (if possible) find something to write about that others have not written extensively about. If that is not possible, you better have a great slant or a different approach or marketing plan – something that really makes your product unique.

☑ **Knowing Your Target Market**

Know your target market. Who will the potential e-book buyers be and how will you attract them to your website, e-book and material?

☑ **Choosing a Topic**

Do not create an e-book about a topic that you are not truly knowledgeable in. I know that may be self-explanatory, but people often like to create e-books about working online and making big bucks from the Internet. Often times those people are not quite experts, so they really should not be creating products that they do not know about. Not only is it dishonest, but also people trust you to provide them with quality information – not to deceive them with false promises.

Step 2: Create Website & Sales Pages

It's important to think about several things. Do you plan to create website(s) to sell your e-book on? Did you do thorough research to find keywords or key phrases to optimize your website for?

Did you look on Clickbank.com and PayDotCom.com to see how much competition you have there or if people are selling similar products?

Since those two affiliate networks are two of the most popular networks to sell and promote e-books and other Digital products on, do you plan to sell yours through there and have affiliates promoting it as well?

☑ **Factors to Consider**

You will need to consider several factors when it comes to creating, marketing and selling your own e-book or product.

This section will guide you through some of the key points to keep in mind. If you decide to have an affiliate program, so others can promote and sell your product for you - there are some measures you should take from the get-go.

So, the reason this section is placed here, rather than after the rest of the tutorials is so that you are aware of other factors that can help or hinder your efforts.

☑ Affiliate Program for Your E-Book

If you do plan to create an affiliate program to sell your e-book on – then you should plan to have two websites. Website #1 will be the website which you optimize for specific keywords relating to the topic of your e-book. That website will contain a lot of keyword-rich quality content with the specific purpose of gaining a high ranking in the search engines and making sales that way. In that website, be sure to follow all of the steps outlined in the Search Engine Optimization Book, located in Book 5.

☑ Two Sales Pages

The reason I recommend that you create a second website is so that the second website's purpose is to be used as a sales page for your affiliates. Your first website is obviously also a sales page for your e-book, but the income you generate from that website will be from targeted search engine traffic that you gain from optimizing your website.

Website #2 differs from the first because you do not want it to be indexed by the search engines. The purpose is to work as a sales page for your e-book – something that is clean, to-the-point and allows your affiliates the ability to promote for you on that website.

This creates two income streams for you. Sometimes it takes a while for your optimized website to gain a high ranking, and in the meantime you should be able to earn an income from the sales that affiliates bring from your second website.

☑ Duplicate Content Warning

The reason your second website cannot be indexed by the search engines is because a lot of the content might be the same as the content on your other website.

The search engines do not look kindly on duplicate content over numerous websites and if you have two websites with the same content – then it is possible that your websites will lose all their ranking and drop from the search engines. That is not something to take a chance on.

In order to allow or disallow the search engines to crawl and index your websites, you must create a robots.txt file and add it to your website.

That is explained in Book 5, Chapter 4.

Be sure to add a robots.txt file that disallows the search engines from indexing your second website, the one that is created for the affiliates to promote.

☑ **Website Essentials**

- Robots.txt file
- Affiliates Link (a link to your "affiliates" page so people know you have an affiliate program, the details of the program, commission payout and structure)
- "About me" page with details of your background, expertise and personal story
- Copyright notice and year of website creation
- Contact form, so people may ask you questions before, during or after buying
- Payment link
- Guarantee or Refund Policy (important)
- Photos and any personal touches really help "sell" yourself and your product

Step 3: E-Book Idea Conceptualization & Writing

Now it is time to layout the ground work and solidify your e-book idea. You should have a clear plan of action to follow regarding what you want the e-book to contain. Solidify your e-book idea and create a clear plan of action to follow regarding writing the e-book. Write the e-book or pay someone on Scriptlance to write it for you, according to your specifications.

☑ **Considerations**

- The length of the e-book
- Your price point for selling the e-book
- Your target market & competition online

Step 4: Formatting the File

The question that I get asked most frequently about e-book creation is what file format or program should be used to create an e-book? I will give you my honest personal recommendation, which is based on my experiences in selling my e-book online. I recommend that you create the file in PDF format.

☑ Issues with .EXE Files

You don't want to create an .exe file format for example (which is quite a popular secondary e-book creation type) because after going through all the work of creating it you will lose all your Macintosh-computer users.

Macintosh's are not compatible with .exe files and in addition to that, most people (even if their computers do allow them to open those file types) do not feel comfortable opening .exe files.

When I first began selling my e-book I created it in .exe file format because with that e-book creation software I used, I was able to set the security preferences so that anytime someone sent the e-book through e-mail to someone (to try to give it away without the person paying) then the e-book would lock up and stop functioning.

That may sound like a good feature but it actually cost me a lot of time and headaches because people oftentimes purchased the e-book while at work, and then wanted to send it to themselves at home or save it to a disc but could not (because it would lock).

It was not worth the hassle for me, so I decided to re-create my e-book in PDF format (allowing the buyers to print the e-book or move it as they like). Although it may sound like a security risk, it seems that I lost more money by wasting all my time answering e-mails and resending download links to frustrated customers.

☑ Converting to a PDF File

Please refer to Book 6, Chapter 3 for PDF conversion and creation software details and information.

☑ Editing & Touching-Up the PDF File

There is one major problem in creating PDF files. If your e-book will contain hyperlinks to other websites you will need to write the hyperlink out in its entirety.

For example, http://www.websitename.com. The problem with this is that some people do not want to write out a long domain name because it may not look professional or pleasing to the eye (or it could be a really long affiliate link that you don't want someone to see too).

You must include the http:// and the rest of the domain, as it will not recognize just domainname.com as a hyperlink.

Sometimes in your e-book text, you may prefer to write, click here to visit this website, with click here hyperlinked. If this is the case, be prepared for some extra touch-up work once the PDF is created.

To edit or alter hyperlinks once your PDF is created, you will need to use a software program to allow you to edit the PDF file. The only program that I have used successfully (and frequently when I do my e-book updates) is CutePDF Professional.

CutePDF Professional

Website: http://honestholly.com/goto/cutepdf �🖈

There is a free trial version available for download and use. You can open up any PDF file in the program to make edits to the hyperlinks, create hyperlinks, and add headers, footers, page numbers, security or digital signatures.

Step 5: Selling Your E-Book Online

Once your e-book is completed, and your sales page(s) are finished, it's time to start selling. Although you may have a website that you are in the process of optimizing, or waiting for it to increase in search engine ranking, you can still sell your e-book online. There are numerous venues that allow e-book authors to share, promote and sell their e-books.

E-bookMall

Website: http://honestholly.com/goto/e-bookmall �🖈

E-bookMall is an excellent website which allows E-Book Creators the ability to sell their e-book online. E-bookMall has a large marketplace full of e-books, grouped by categories. For each sale made, the E-Book Creator keeps part of the profits, and agrees to give E-bookMall part of the profits. This way, the E-Book Creator gets free exposure for the sale. There is absolutely no work involved (as E-bookMall does the entire sales process) so it is a great option to increase e-book sales.

Clickbank

Website: http://honestholly.com/goto/clickbank �🖈

Clickbank is another popular digital goods marketplace in which you can list and sell your e-book. You can also sign-up to allow affiliates promote for you, and earn commissions for each sale.

Plimus

Website: http://honestholly.com/goto/plimus ✑

Plimus is my favorite place to sell and promote my e-book. It is my favorite because it seems to have more features, flexibility and ease-of-use than anything I have used before. It also has advanced tracking and statistics, which enables sellers to track which hits are leading to sales. It will help the seller know which campaigns are selling, which sales pages need improvement and where the traffic is coming from. Plimus has incredible customer support, and allows e-book sellers the opportunity to have affiliates to promote for them.

Redirecting to Product Download

After someone purchases your e-book, then he should be given immediate access to it, either by e-mail or redirecting him to a download page. Most of the e-book sales websites, offer a secure service so that the buyer will be given access to the product purchased (once the payment is verified). Payment verification generally takes a few seconds, to a few minutes.

With Plimus.com, for example, if you are vendor, then you can upload your e-book or product. After a purchase is successfully made, and verified – the purchaser will be e-mailed a direct link to download it. The download will be safe and secure in Plimus's system.

But, if you use Clickbank, for example, you will need to provide an actual download page for the product. That download page would need to be on your own web hosting server or website. Book 6, Chapter 3, explains how to create a secure download page.

CHAPTER 2: SELF-PUBLISHING YOUR E-BOOK

Although people love having the freedom to buy downloadable e-books, there is still a large group of people in the world who prefer paperbacks or hard-cover books. Not everyone enjoys being on the computer at all times of the day, and it can be quite nice to take an actual book into the hands and read outside or in bed.

From Download to Physical Delivery

Presently, it is easier than ever to take your e-book or downloadable report, and sell it as a paperback or hard-cover.

With self-publishing, you basically upload your e-book file(s). Then, you select what type of binding you would like, what type of paper quality, color or black and white, and several other specifications. After setting up your product specifications, you will be advised on how much it will cost for the printing of one book.

The total cost might be $5 USD for a one-hundred page book. After knowing the price per book, you can then raise the price to whatever you prefer. If you want to sell your book for $15 USD, you can. Once someone makes a purchase, the self-publishing company will do all of the work involved in publishing and shipping out your book.

You will immediately earn a set amount of money or percentage of profits per sale. If you noticed, other than uploading a file, you had no other work involved with that entire process. No overhead costs or shipping costs. The online company which offers this incredible service is Lulu.

Website: http://honestholly.com/goto/lulu ✈

LuLu.com's Self Publishing

Lulu's self-publishing services have become widely respected and known globally. Lulu provides what they call "creators" with the ability to easily upload, manage settings and sell. That's it. Creators can sell their own written work, publish in hard-cover or paperback, and create photo books or calendars and even CDs. Lulu simplifies the process for creators of these products, who have very little to worry about once the files are uploaded. Lulu takes 20% commission and also offers a huge array of self-publishing services and marketing assistance.

☑ ISBN Number

A new service that caught my attention right away was their "Published by You Service," which allows individuals to obtain valid legal ISBN numbers for their published work. An ISBN Number is an internationally recognized identification code, which basically opens up all possibilities in selling your product anywhere in the world. It also means that your published book will be listed in all of the major global book industry databases, according to Lulu. The price for this service (as of 2008) is $99.95 USD.

☑ Eligibility

To be eligible to obtain an ISBN number for your published work, you will need to meet a few standards which relate to book binding and pages. According to Lulu's website, Lulu has partnered with print vendors for printing books on demand when orders are placed by booksellers such as Amazon.com, Barnes & Noble and independent stores and libraries.

☑ Remarks

My personal experiences with Lulu have been wonderful. I have not had any payment issues or problems receiving any items I have purchased. I appreciate how "global" the website truly is because it opens the doors to so many opportunities. I was previously living outside of the USA, and just the fact that I could purchase and have items delivered to me in Thailand was a plus. The delivery was fast and charges for shipping were very reasonable. The quality of the books published has been the same, if not better than any book I have purchased locally.

CHAPTER 3: CLOTHING & BRAND CREATION

Did you know that not only can you become a published author online, but you can also design and sell clothes and other items? The concepts used in the self-publishing platform (with Lulu) are similar to the ones with selling clothing. Basically, you can either create several graphics or designs, or pay someone to do that. Then login and upload those graphics. Then you choose what items you want them to be displayed on. You are given a base price. Any amount that you charge, above that price is what you will earn per sale item (minus fees). When people purchase, the items are created and shipped out, so you have absolutely no involvement in the "work."

Cafepress Product Creation

Cafepress is an amazing place for creative people to share their creativity with the world (and make a profit). You can join for free, and start selling right away. Basically, you sign-up for a free account, and then you can go to: "Create Shop," to start your first shop.

You will be given a unique URL or website address that you can use to direct traffic to your shop. I have created my first shop and named it "Save Burma," because I want to sell clothing related to the War in Burma, and spread awareness on the topic.

Whatever you decide to create a shop about is entirely up to you. It can be a topic related to your niche, or basically anything that interests you personally.

☑ Creating a Graphic to Use

Creating a graphic image to use and upload is going to be the most difficult part for users. Not everyone is artistically inclined or enjoys graphic design. Not everyone can afford to purchase expensive graphic design software. But there are simple solutions and alternatives to this.

First, the best software I have ever used (for graphics and photos and design) is Adobe Photoshop. The cost is a bit high and the features are incredible. It is not overly user-friendly for non-experienced users. When I first began using it years ago, I was totally lost. If you have the program, and you have the patience – go for it. If not, there is an excellent alternative that is totally free – Gimp.

Commercial Pro Graphics Design Software

Adobe Photoshop http://honestholly.com/goto/photoshop 📌

Adobe Photoshop is a feature-rich software program for photographers, graphic designs, web designers, and anyone who is interested in advanced image editing and features. There is a free trial available.

Free Professional Graphics Design Software

Gimp http://honestholly.com/goto/gimp 📌

Gimp is a totally free alternative to Adobe Photoshop. It will give you a vast range of image-editing abilities, with ease-of-use. I highly recommend this program, and I have used it installed on my computer (even though I have Photoshop as well – it is that good).

Size of Graphic for CafePress

If you are creating a graphic or image to upload to CafePress, there are no standard specifications for file size. Personally, I have created images that were approximately 700 pixels in height, by 500 pixels wide. I had no problems with that particular image size.

In either Image editing program listed above, you can go to: "New" then "File" and specify file size and background (which can be white or transparent). I generally choose white. After creating my simple "Save Burma" graphic, I have uploaded it.

Different Product Choices

The screenshot on the next page contains several of the items I chose to promote in my "Save Burma" shop. I uploaded two other graphics which said "Save Burma" so I could test their popularity and only keep the ones which are selling.

After uploading your graphic, you can choose how high you want your price mark-up to be. I made my price $2 USD higher than the cost to create and ship it. So, for each item sold, I will earn $2 USD.

MORE COLORS AVAILABLE

Save Burma Women's
Light T-Shirt
$16.99

Save Burma Dog T-Shirt
$15.99

MORE COLORS AVAILABLE

Save Burma Jr. Raglar
$19.99

MORE COLORS AVAILABLE

Save Burma Women's
Cap Sleeve T-Shirt
$17.99

Save Burma Jr. Hoodie
$26.99

MORE COLORS AVAILABLE

Save Burma Baseball
Jersey
$18.99

Here you can see the products which I am selling in my "Save Burma" store. There are additional product choices and you can brand your graphic on a variety of different items.

Setting Prices & Making Money

After logging into your account area, you can manage your shops, view your earnings and add or edit items. In this screenshot you can see that I have $18 USD in CafeCash. This means I have earned $18 USD in profits from my "Save Burma" shop. Please see screenshot on the following page.

If you open up a shop, be sure that you set the price point right after you upload your graphic(s) and choose your products to sell. CafePress allows you to create multiple shops (totally free) and I did this one time and forgot to raise the price per item. It lets you specify price per item or in bulk – how much you want the price raised above the standard.

So, I personally chose $2 USD higher than the standard price. But, when I first opened up my shop, I forgot to set the price. I lost a lot of possible sales - $2 dollars here and $2 dollars there. It adds up. Don't forget to set the price.

I created the shop on a whim, due to a personal passion for raising awareness of the war. I did not realize how the political situation in the country would be changing. So, with the ever-changing crisis, the sales seem to be increasing.

So, if you choose a popular topic or something that is news-worthy or even controversial – you could get more sales. It depends on quite a few factors, but either way it is a simple way to increase possible revenue (and learn while you're doing it).

BOOK 8

Advanced Monetization Methods

CHAPTER 1: VISUAL CARD DIRECTORY

Methods to monetize your profits online have taken an extreme turn, making it much easier for the average Joe marketer to strike it big. The advanced website applications and programs that are freely available to you provide you with tools that would have cost you thousands of dollars in the past. Now, the tools are provided to you for free and all you need to do is get a little website traffic to earn money. Some of the things you are already doing online (for example, posting videos on Youtube or writing on your Myspace page). The exact things that you may already be doing (to keep family and friends updated with your life status) could be earning you money! Monetization methods have taken an extreme "Web 2.0" turn – becoming highly interactive, free-to-use and earn big.

Blast Free Ad Network

Website: http://honestholly.com/goto/blast

Blast is an ad network that allows you to advertise and receive targeted visitors to your website(s) for free. The "normal" directory website is comprised of categories which contain lists of website links, and a description of the particular website. This directory differs because it is visual, with user-submitted ads. If you would like to use the service, you can join and use it for free. Once you login, you can submit your ad to the directory. It must be 270 pixels by 165 pixels in size.

Users can login at any time to view statistics about the ad – number of clicks and where the ad is placed (for example, category: businesses, page 2). It is totally free to use the service, but if you want to guarantee that your ad will show up on the 1st page, you can pay a certain amount of money per day to make that happen. The price per day varies, according to the competition and the number of ads. At one time I paid 30 cents per day, for 30 days ($9 USD) to have my ad show up on the first page. The price will increase or decrease as time passes.

Benefits & Purpose

One major benefit of creating and posting visual ads (besides the obvious, which is the website exposure) is that you are creating a link back to your main website. This is very important for SEO. When you create your ad and are ready to submit it, you can "tag" it or put it under certain categories. The categories or tags are user-created.

So, I created a category for "Honest Riches" and one for "Holly Mann" and also submitted the ad to business, marketing, internet marketing and several others. Once this was done, the website automatically created URLs for the new category. So, not only did I receive on high quality link back to my website, but also several more (because each category or tag also added a new page to the blast website, which linked to my website). So, if I just created a website and wanted it to be indexed by the search engines right away, this is another good way to make it happen quickly. Another benefit is that you can post as many ads as you like. You can link the ads to any websites that you want (and that means you can use a direct affiliate link as well).

Statistics & Profits

Once you login to the admin area of the Blast site, you can view the statistics for your visual ads. The statistics will tell you how many views the ad has received, how many clicks it has received and the click-through rate (percentage).

Blast Widget & Referrals

In addition to the high quality links and free targeted traffic, you also have the opportunity to earn more money from the website. Once logged into the admin area of the site, you can click on the tab for "My Account," & then click on another link that says Referral Link. You can use the referral link to tell others about the website. People love free advertising so if they sign-up and decide to pay for extra exposure (to have their ad on the front page, for example) then you will earn a 50% affiliate commission from all referred sales. You can also click on the tab that says "Add the Blast Widget," to quickly create a widget for your website or blog. A widget is a piece of self-contained code, and once created, it will update itself by rotating ads (while on your website or blog).

How to Add a Widget to Your Website

☑ **Wordpress**

- First, specify (on the Blast site) how you would like your widget to look, then copy the code (CTRL+A and then CTRL+C)
- Login to the Wordpress admin area, scroll over the "design" tab & click "widgets"
- View all of the available widgets on the left-hand side
- Find the widget that says "Text" and click the link next to it that says "Add" – only click this once
- Look to the right-hand side of your page where it says "Current Widgets," and see that there is a new tab there at the bottom – "Text"
- Scroll over it, click on "Edit" & paste in the code that you copied earlier & save
- View your website in a new window to see the widget

☑ **HTML Website**

- If you have created a standard HTML-based website, just open up the program that you use to edit and create content
- Make sure you have copied the widget code from the Blast site (CTRL+A and CTRL+C)
- If you want the widget to appear on the right side of your page, and you already have a sidebar, just locate the spot you want to place it into
- Go into the "code view" and paste the code into that spot
- Save the file and view it online to see if it is where you want it to show up

☑ **PHP Website**

- Login to your file management area or the program you use to create pages
- Make sure you have copied the widget code from the Blast site (CTRL+A and CTRL+C)
- Create a new page and name it anything that you like, for example: blast.php
- Paste the widget code (from the Blast site) into the blast.php file and save it

- Go into your homepage's template file – it could be index.php or home.php
- Find the exact location where you want the widget to appear, and view the code
- When you know where you want the widget to appear, you will need to use the PHP Include function like this:

  <?php include("blast.php"); ?>
- Save the files and view the website to see that the widget is in the correct place

CHAPTER 2: AMAZON ASSOCIATES

Joining & Benefits

Amazon is an American e-commerce company which launched online in 1995. It grew from being an online bookstore, to offering a diversified array of products and global shipping on many of them. The Amazon Associates program was created to allow people to earn cash by promoting Amazon products online. Whether you have a small blog, website or an enormous following online, the program can be used as a monetization tool.

The income-potential with Amazon's Associates program is enormous. The affiliate tools you are provided with make it simple to incorporate it into your current website or blog. According to Wikipedia, the revenue for Amazon in 2007 was more than 14.8 billion USD.

It's incredible to think that Amazon has opened its doors to allow regular people to promote their products. I am glad we can take part in such a huge income-generating program.

The program allows you to earn up to 15% in referral fees by linking to any products or services offered on Amazon. For More Information & To Join the Amazon Associates Program, please visit the link below.

Amazon Associates Program Details
Website: http://honestholly.com/goto/amazon 📌

Amazon Widgets Galore

The Associates Program offers a wide range of widgets that you can easily integrate into your current website or blog. The methods of inserting the widget into your website are the same as in Book 8, Chapter 1.

☑ Types of Widgets

- Page Recommender Widget
- MP3 Clips Widgets & Carousel Widget
- Your Video Widget
- Deals Widget & Product Clouds
- Unbox Videos or Slideshows
- My Favorites & Wish List
- Quick Linker & Search
- Product Links & Banners

☑ Specific Product Link Widgets

If you want to create a link to a specific product, just login and click on: "Classic Links" and then "Product Links." You will be taken to a new screen which allows you to search for the specific product you want to link to. Once you find the product, you can then customize the appearance of the link and widget.

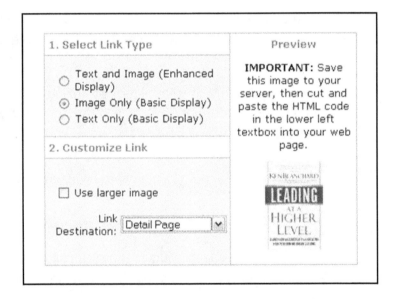

Building a Specific Product Link in Amazon Associates

Creating Your AStore

Once you are an Amazon Associate, another benefit of the program is having the ability to create your own Amazon stores (AStores) and integrate them into your websites. You can fill the store with any products that you choose, and even brand it and incorporate it to fit the appearance and theme of your current website.

Basically, Amazon gives you the ability to create your very own online store, with absolutely no programming experience needed (and it is also free). Users can have up to 100 AStores per account. The earnings and statistics are all handled through your Amazon Associates account area.

☑ Integration Options

After choosing to create your AStore, you will be walked through a series of steps which allow you to customize the products you want to have in your store. You can choose products according to a certain category or sub-category, or you can hand-pick the items you want to have in the store. After choosing products, you will be able to customize how you want the store to look.

You will be able to change the background color, hyperlink colors and other visual elements of the store. Personally, I created my AStore and integrated it to have the same background color as my website, and similar text and fonts as well.

You will have three options to integrate the AStore into your website. You can get a simple link to your store, which will stand alone and can be used anywhere. Or, you can get the code to embed the store using an inline frame or a frameset. The last two options are what I would recommend you use – so that your store is totally integrated into your website's theme and looks like your own store.

For myself, I prefer to use Wordpress for most of my websites and the problem with integration is that the sidebar (in my regular Wordpress website) takes up too much space. I want to have that extra space for my AStore and also make the store page as clean as possible. So, in order to remove the sidebar and place the AStore into a Wordpress website, I need to create a Wordpress template file that does not contain the sidebar. Not everyone is aware of this, but when you login to your Wordpress Admin area and you want to create a page, you have the option to use a specific page template. So, you will need to create one for the AStore to integrate smoothly into your website.

Advanced AStore Integration for Wordpress

- First, you will need to login to your web hosting account area for your website (or login to a FTP program or some other program that allows file uploads or editing). You had a visual guide on how to do this in Book 5, Chapter 5 (The tutorial on Bluehost and Wordpress One-Click Plug-In Installation).

- Once you are logged into your File Management area, you will need to navigate to the folder which contains your Wordpress theme files (the theme that you have activated and are currently using).

    - The location of my theme files are: /public_html/wp-content/themes/revolutionpro/ (the name of my theme folder is revolutionpro).

- Once inside the folder which contains all of your active theme files, you will need to create a new file. The file will be a template file. It is only necessary to create this if your website has a sidebar that is being used. The problem with the sidebar is that when you want to integrate your AStore, there is very little space if you already have a sidebar there.

    - You can create the new file in notepad or else create it within your file management area.
    - Or, feel free to use my page_noside.php file (the exact same template file I created & use) here: http://honestholly.com/goto/pagenoside. ✦
    - Just download the file to your computer and save it. Then upload it directly into your active theme folder as listed above.

- Next, login to your Wordpress admin area and scroll over "Write" then "Page."

- Scroll down below the text box area and you will see advanced options.

- One option you will see is "Page Template," and just click on the box and view the available templates.

- At this time (since you already uploaded the new template, page_noside.php), you should see a file that is named: Page NoSidebar – click to highlight and use that one when you are ready to integrate your AStore.

Advanced Options for Page Templates in Wordpress

- Now, you are totally ready to integrate your AStore into your Wordpress website. The page you are creating for your store will show up within your website navigation. I named my page for my AStore – "Success Shop."

- Next, you will need to login to your Amazon AStore account area, finish up your AStore customizations and get your store link.

- Choose the option that allows you to "Embed My Store In An Inline Frame," and you will receive a piece of code similar to this:

  <iframe src="http://astore.amazon.com/honeholl-20" width="90%" height="4000" frameborder="0" scrolling="no"></iframe>

- Copy that piece of code, and insert it into the page you are creating for your store. You may need to click HTML or HTML View to insert it directly into the text editor while creating the page.

- Be sure to check the "Advanced Option" below the text editor and choose "Page Template," – then "Page NoSidebar," and you're done.

- Save your Wordpress page and view it to be sure it looks alright. If you have any issues with how the AStore looks, you can login to your Amazon Associates account area and edit the store (to change the size of elements or colors and fonts).

☑ **Honest Holly Success Shop Integration**

The following screenshot shows the final result I received for my AStore after following the steps I detailed in the Advanced AStore Integration for Wordpress. The final result that you will receive will vary, depending on how you choose to customize the appearance of the store in your Amazon Associates AStore editing area.

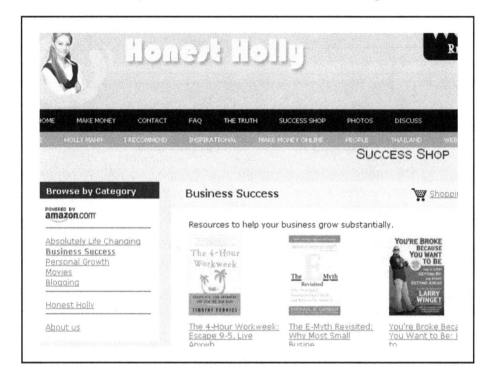

☑ Complete Integration of Colors - Tip

The seamless integration of colors between my Wordpress theme and the AStore was done with one simple Firefox Extension – ColorZilla.

It is one of my favorite extensions, as I use it so often with website design. Once installed, I just click on the tiny tool in the left-hand bottom corner of my browser. It gives me an advanced eye dropper or color picker to take any color off of any website. I scroll over the background color of my theme (which is the identical color I want for the background of my AStore) and then I copy the color code: #FFE7B2 and insert it in while customizing my AStore design and colors.

Download ColorZilla
Website: http://honestholly.com/goto/colorzilla ✈

Monetize Your Videos with Amazon

Another incredible new method to making money with Amazon's Associates program is through the "Your Video," widget. First, you can use any video for this; personal, family-related or marketing-type videos.

The widget will allow you to upload videos or use videos that you already have online, and insert in Amazon product links or information to link the viewer to Amazon. Whenever a person clicks through the link and makes a purchase of any Amazon products, you will earn commissions in your Associates account.

Just login to your Amazon Associates account area, click on "Build Links and Widgets" and a new page will open. The new page will provide you with an assortment of widget choices – just click on "Your Video Widget."

☑ **Uploading Your Video**

- The video you upload must be in one of the accepted formats: avi, flv, mov, mpg or wmv.

- When ready to upload, you will be able to select a video from your computer and click the Upload button. It may take a few minutes to process.

☑ **Product Pop-Ups**

- Once your video is fully uploaded, you can then create product pop-ups or overlays to place within the video.

- You can insert as many Amazon ads or product pop-ups as you like, as long as they are not within 10 seconds of each other (please note this may change, so you should verify the rules and restrictions once you are logged into your account).

☑ **Viral Videos & Amazon Profits**

- After creating your video widget, you will receive a piece of code so you can easily embed it within your website.

- Videos are viral and if you have something entertaining or useful to share, it can be spread from person-to-person quite quickly.

- If other people post your video to their website, you will earn money.

Video Reviews

A useful approach to utilizing the "Your Video" widgets with Amazon is to create short video reviews. Whoever views the videos, is a targeted prospective customer (or else he would not be watching it).

Or, even if you send the link to your video to family and friends, they could end up making some type of purchase on the Amazon website and you would earn the referral cash.

CHAPTER 3: SOCIAL NETWORK REVENUE SHARING

How It Works

Social networking, as explained in Book 3, Chapter 4, is a widely used platform for people who want to interact with like-minded individuals, join groups and discussions, and also maintain a personal blog and add photos and videos. Much of the world; both young and old are a part of some type of social network. There is a revolutionary Social Network called Flixya, and it offers all of its members a 100% ad revenue share program.

The average social network online has ads placed on each user's profile page, blog and on every other page imaginable. This is a huge revenue source for the creators of the website, but can be annoying at times to the users. The fact is, most of the social networks online will continue using ads as a means to monetize their website and cover basic expenses. So, Flixya is a social network that differs because it offers all users the opportunity to earn 100% ad revenue sharing.

Flixya – Share Everything

Flixya is a social network which allows those who join, to input their Google Adsense information to earn an income while using the website.

Flixya

Website: http://honestholly.com/goto/flixya

Upon joining the website, you will be asked if you have a Google Adsense account and if you want to take part in the revenue-sharing. If you click "yes" to that option, then Flixya will ask you for your Google Adsense information. Basically, you are giving the external website (Flixya) permission to associate your Google Adsense account with the website, in order to give credit to you for all of your ads and revenue. Your account management pages allow you to add-to or edit your profile, images, photos, blogs, galleries and subscriptions.

Whenever you upload images, videos or post to your blog or personal page, you are eligible to earn more revenue. Google Adsense ads will be placed on the pages where you add content, images or videos. Whenever viewers (other than yourself) click on any Google Adsense ads, you will profit. You can track the earnings and view all the details by logging into your Google Adsense account. All of your earnings are managed through there.

Understanding Adsense Revenue Sharing

It's important that people are aware of the potential profits involved with Google Adsense Revenue Sharing. Google Adsense is a program that is widely known among Internet Marketers and non-marketers alike. Although it is well-known, it's important to be open-minded and realistic about earnings. That way, if the Adsense ads are not earning you enough revenue, you could try replacing them with different ads (from Adbrite or another website).

First, the amount of money that you may or may not earn with the ads varies greatly and depends on several factors; the number of clicks, the type of ad and the competition online for the advertisers. Personally, I have quite a few websites online and many of which incorporate Google Adsense ads into them. The profits are generally $200 USD to $300 USD per month total (for all of my website Adsense earnings combined).

If you would like to review the average earnings for websites which fall into a particular category (such as; business, health, fitness or marketing) you can do so through AdMoolah. The website provides detailed statistics and comparisons of ads, websites and their earnings with Google Adsense ads. It is helpful to understand your competition online, and to know more about what it takes to increase your earnings.

AdMoolah
Website: http://honestholly.com/goto/admoolah

CHAPTER 4: CASH FOR THE CREATIVE

MetaCafe Producer Rewards

Metacafe is one of the largest and highly trafficked video websites online. After joining the website, you can begin submitting videos.

If you are a creative person and upload something that attracts quite a few views and visits – you can earn cash. MetaCafe gives credit to all video producers who upload something that attracts a lot of views. You could upload a video that you edited or touched up to make it funny. Or, you could have just had great luck and stumbled upon something extraordinarily funny. Either way, you can make money from it.

MetaCafe
Website: http://honestholly.com/goto/metarewards ✄

Entertain to Gain

If you submit a video to Metacafe, and it has the power to entertain the masses, you will earn money.

- For 20,000 views, you will earn $100 USD.
- For 200,000 views, you will earn $1,000 USD.
- For 2 million views, you will earn $10,000 USD.

Video-Editing Software for Free

If you want to edit a video you already have, Memories On Web is a free software program that I have had excellent experiences with using. I have tried several other programs (commercial) which were costly and difficult to use. Memories on Web is free to download and is an excellent way to edit videos (for home or business use).

Memories On Web
Website: http://honestholly.com/goto/memoriesonweb ✄

Youtube Community Contests

The Youtube Community is an area of the Youtube which provides users with the opportunity to participate in on-going contests. Obviously, this isn't a surefire way to create an income, but it is a fun way to try to make extra cash. Big brand-name companies and manufacturers are turning to the internet to create buzz for their products, while getting users involved. The contest examples listed below are actual contests that have been on the Youtube Community page. Checkout the current contests by visiting the link below.

Youtube Community
Website: http://honestholly.com/goto/youtubecontests 📌

Several examples of actual Youtube Community Contests include:

Circuit City "Take My TV Contest"
- Users upload videos of their terrible television, speakers and home entertainment system
- The best video of the worst home television setup receives the ultimate HDTV & home theater package

SanDisk's "Point & Shoot Film Festival Contest"
- Users submit a two-minute action shot from a point-and-shoot camera (no camcorders) with the theme of "Life Moves," with no edits allowed
- Grand-Prize Winner receives $10,000 USD & a trip to Las Vegas, NV
- Winners of categories receive $1000 USD & more prizes

Walmart's "Moms Can Do Anything Contest"
- Users submit videos which include useful money-saving tips
- 10 Grand-Prize Winners receive a year's worth of groceries from Walmart

CHAPTER 5: TEXT LINK ADS

Targeted Text-Link Traffic

Text-Link-Ads is a targeted traffic and link popularity ad firm. They serve both publishers as well as advertisers who want to publish ads on related websites. If you are a publisher, you will be paid a set amount per month, per advertisement. For those who purchase the text-link advertisements, it is a reassurance to know that the price is final and does not vary depending on the number of clicks received or amount of traffic (many websites charge in this way and it is costly).

Text-Link-Ads

Website: http://honestholly.com/goto/textlinkads 📌

As a publisher, it only took me five minutes to sign-up and complete the steps to earning with the program.

- First, you sign-up and submit your website address.
- Next, provide website details & summary about your website.
- Finally, you will receive a piece of code to insert into your website.

Once you complete the basic steps listed above, you will receive a confirmation e-mail from the website to let you know if you have been approved and if the code you inserted into your website was entered in correctly. I managed to accomplish all of those steps within five minutes. Once done, you must be patient as it can take a day or two before any ads appear on your website. Do not delete the code that you inserted (thinking it may not be working properly) rather, just be patient and check back at your website later.

Profits & Earning-Potential

According to the Text-Link-Ads website, publishers will receive 50% of the sale price for each text link ad sold off your website through their system. Their ad-serving technology supports websites that are html-based, PHP, ASP, PERL, Ruby on Rails, forums, Wordpress blogs and many more. Their website interface makes it pretty easy for non-technical savvy users to accomplish the task of inserting in the small piece of code.

 If you have any problems or issues doing so, the Text-Link-Ads website offers free tutorials and even a Link Buying Guide (packed full of excellent linking strategies information and SEO techniques). Those can be downloaded once you are logged into the admin area.

Experiences

As I mentioned earlier, I signed-up with Text-Link-Ads and within five minutes I completed all of the required steps.

I received a confirmation e-mail and details stating I would earn between $10 USD and $25 USD per month per link. Through their service, they sell a maximum of 4 links on one page and they have a 50% revenue share policy.

So, the site can make between $20.00 and $50.00 per month if all 4 ad spots are filled with advertisers. According to the Text-Link-Ads website, the final pricing is set in accordance with current market demand (and may vary).

If you have multiple websites, you can increase your earnings and income streams significantly. Several major affiliate marketers and professional bloggers I know of make the majority of their earnings (from their blogs) with Text-Link-Ads.

Book 9

IM Tookit

CHAPTER 1: FREE SOFTWARE PRIMER

In my Internet marketing career, I have purchased countless numbers of web design tools, add-ons and paid for programming when I could have gotten it all for free. Too often people starting their venture online spend entirely too much money on costly software and tools. It is not necessary as nearly everything can be used for free.

Sharing Technology Freely

Previously, I was completely unaware of a huge subculture online of techies, programmers, developers and web designers who are part of a group, which believes in sharing technological advances freely.

For example, a programmer might create a modern, high-tech flash gallery plug-in for a regular website. If he/she decides to create it as an open source project, that means others may use it for free, modify the code and do what they want with it.

☑ **Open Source Licensed Software**

The reason they share their work openly with the public is so that others may use the source code (the actual html, php, databases or other programming languages used to create it) so that the software may be changed, may evolve and become better. Because so many programmers can edit and update, fix bugs and make changes – the software quickly improves in functions, capabilities and features.

Generally, when someone creates this type of software, one which allows complete code access to the public, it is considered "open source." Open source software must comply with a set of criteria to be licensed as open source.

According to the Open Source Initiative, http://honestholly.com/goto/opensourcedoc ✔ certain criteria must be met for something to be considered open source.

☑ **Open Source Software Licenses Requirements**

- Free Distribution
- Source Code
- Integrity of Author's Source Code
- No Discrimination Against Persons or Groups
- Distribution of License
- License Must Not Be Specific to a Product
- License Must Not Restrict Other Software
- License Must Be Technology Neutral
- Further definitions and explanations of that criterion can be found at: http://honestholly.com/goto/opensourcedoc 📌

The Free Software Foundation
Website: http://honestholly.com/goto/fsf 📌

- Established in 1985
- Dedicated to promoting computer users' rights to use, study, copy, modify, and redistribute computer programs
- Directory of 4,000+ Free Software Programs here: http://honestholly.com/goto/fsfdirect 📌
- Examples include: e-mail, games, video, live communications, printing, business

Savannah
Website: http://honestholly.com/goto/savannah 📌

- Partner website of Free Software Foundation
- Offers information and searchable open source works (on left-hand side of site)

Sourceforge
Website: http://honestholly.com/goto/sourceforge 📌

- One of the most popular websites, which offers a comprehensive list of projects and download links for open source works.
- There are tens of thousands of free tools – and an option to search through them by keyword or browsing the categories
- Free software categories include: desktop, development, financial, games, hardware, networking, security, storage, VOIP, etc.

Different Types of Free Software

There are different types of licenses and terms for "free" software, and each one should be understood (especially if you decide to redistribute or edit any code). Confusing conflicting or similarly-related terms for different licenses for "free" software leave many people feeling uneasy.

The section will attempt to clarify the differences and offer you a basic definition of each type of "free" software. If overwhelmed with confusion (and you don't plan to actually edit or distribute items) then feel free to skim over or skip this section. The creators of the Free Software Foundation have attempted to clarify the meanings and terms. According to their website, http://honestholly.com/goto/gnu ⬐ several types of licenses exist for "free" software.

Free Software
Free software is software that comes with permission for anyone to use, copy, and distribute, either verbatim or with modifications, either gratis or for a fee. In particular, this means that source code must be available.

Open Source Software
The term "open source" software is used by some people to mean more or less the same category as free software. Nearly all free software is open source, and nearly all open source software is free.

Public Domain Software
Public domain software is software that is not copyrighted. Most free software is not in the public domain; it is copyrighted, and the copyright holders have legally given permission for everyone to use it in freedom, using a free software license.

Copylefted Software
Copylefted software is free software whose distribution terms ensure that all copies of all versions are free software. This means, for instance, that copyleft licenses generally disallow others to add additional requirements to the software (though a limited set of safe added requirements can be allowed) and require making source code available.

Non-Copylefted Free Software
Non-copylefted free software comes from the author with permission to redistribute and modify, and also to add additional restrictions to it. If a program is free but not copylefted, then some copies or modified versions may not be free at all.

GPL-covered software

The GNU GPL (General Public License) is one specific set of distribution terms for copylefting a program. The GNU Project uses it as the distribution terms for most GNU software.

GNU software

GNU software is released under the support of the GNU Project. If a program is GNU software, we also say that it is a GNU program or a GNU package. The README or manual of a GNU package should say it is one; also, the Free Software Directory indentifies all GNU packages. All GNU software must be free software.

Freeware

The term "freeware" has no clear definition, but it is commonly used for packages which permit redistribution but not modification (and their source code is not available). These packages are not free software, so please don't use "freeware" to refer to free software.

Shareware

Shareware is software which comes with permission for people to redistribute copies, but says that anyone who continues to use a copy is required to pay a license fee. Shareware is not free software, or even semi-free.

CHAPTER 2: FREE SOFTWARE

Project Planning & Brainstorming

FreeMind

FreeMind is software that keeps track of projects, tasks and subtasks. Good for brainstorming, research, essay writing and note collection.

Website:
http://honestholly.com/goto/freemind

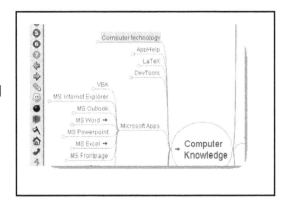

PHProjekt

PHProjekt is software for the coordination of group activities and to share information and documents.
Features of PHProjekt: Group calendar, project management, time card system, file management, contact manager, mail client more.

Website:
http://honestholly.com/goto/phprojekt

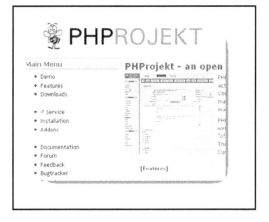

Free Website Design Templates

Free CSS Templates
Website: http://honestholly.com/goto/freecsstemp 📌

Modern Free Table-less CSS Templates
Website: http://honestholly.com/goto/morefreecss 📌

Open Source Web Design (OSWD)
Website: http://honestholly.com/goto/oswd 📌

Stunning Open Source Templates
Website: http://honestholly.com/goto/opensourcetemplates 📌

Free Wordpress Themes

FreeWPThemes.net
Website: http://honestholly.com/goto/freewpthemes 📌

Blog Oh Blog
Website: http://honestholly.com/goto/blogohblog 📌

100 Excellent Wordpress Themes
Website: http://honestholly.com/goto/bestthemes 📌

Free Scripts

Dynamic Drive

Website: http://honestholly.com/goto/dynamicdrive 📌

Huge script library, to provide you with the codes and scripts needed to increase your website functionality and features. Script categories include: calendars, date & time, document effects, dynamic content (ajax), form effects, games, image effects, links & tooltips, menus & navigation, XML & RSS, and more. Some scripts are simple to use, and other require a little bit more work to set up. It's a good way to familiarize you with other aspects of design. Each script includes a demo example on the Dynamic Drive website, with code (any images it includes) and instructions.

DHTML Goodies

Website: http://honestholly.com/goto/dhtml 📌

Another large free script library, including DHTML and AJAX scripts. DHTML stands for Dynamic HTML – and each time the web content is viewed, it may change (or is dynamic). The change can be based upon either: location of the reader, if the reader has viewed the page already from a particular computer and other details about the profile of the reader. Ajax stands for asynchronous JavaScript and XML, and is used for creating interactive web applications. With Ajax, web applications can retrieve data from the server asynchronously in the background without interfering with web page.

For example, if you click a regular website link, you may need to wait as another page on the site loads and displays. But, with Ajax-loaded pages, if you click to view another link, you will quickly see the page change (without redirecting or refreshing).

Advanced Scripts for Free

Dolphin Social Network Script

Website: http://honestholly.com/goto/dolphinsoft ✒

This is a free social networking script which allows you to create a fully-interactive community; with user blogs, photo albums, voting, songs, images and more. Multiple

languages are supported, and there is an optional integration of phpBB forum or vBulletin forum (default is the Orca forum script).

It is a complete social network, one which some have compared to "Myspace," due to the extensive features. Affiliate system with commissions tracking routine and security tools (you can specify privileges for types of memberships which you create, either allowing free access or accepting membership payments).

Media Wiki

Website: http://honestholly.com/goto/mediawikisetup ✒

This is an advanced wiki script that can be downloaded and used for free. It was originally written for Wikipedia. According to Wikipedia, a "wiki" is a collection of web pages which are designed to allow any readers to also be contributors. It makes everyone an author who can edit or add content. So, the Media Wiki script that can be used and downloaded for free, gives you the ability to have your own "wiki" site of some sort (on any topic or range of topics you prefer).

If you want to create a "wiki" site that specializes in topics only related to your niche, this could give your site a high authority and ranking online. It would create a lot of content which could be picked up by the search engines. From personal experiences, when I am looking for information about a topic online, Wikipedia (as well as other wiki sites) usually have the top ranking. Maybe it is due to the built-in SEO features and clean coding.

Free Fonts

Dafont

Website: http://honestholly.com/goto/freefonts ⚓

When it comes to dealing with graphics and any sort of web design (even just editing a basic photo for a text logo), fonts can make a world of a difference. Fonts can "make" or "break" your design and give your business a little extra edge above the rest. Downloading them for free, to use for your logo, can also save you cash.

Example Fonts:

Hand of Sean

Chopin Script

☑ **How to Install Fonts:**

If you have never installed a font, there are several methods to do this easily. The methods vary depending on your computer's operating system. First, just download the font file (normally it is in a zip file) to your computer. Then follow the instructions below. Please read the readme.txt file if it includes one. It will be a message from the font designer, with any restrictions that might be in place with the usage of the font. If in doubt, contact the designer to clarify.

- Windows Vista : Right-click on the font files > "Install"
- Windows XP : Put the font files into C:\Windows\Fonts
- Mac OS X : Double-click the font file > "Install font" button

Images & Graphics

Stock.xchng Free Stock Photos

Website: http://honestholly.com/goto/freeimages

This is a website which allows users to download stock images (professional graphics) to use for free. If you would only like to use the image or graphics that you download, for web design purposes, on websites, presentations, in printed promotional materials, that is allowed.

Please read the legal agreement before using anything in printed material (Example, with CafePress). According to their legal agreement, as of 2008 – it states that you should ask permission of the creator of the image if you want to use their image on "print on demand" items. Please use discretion and if in doubt, as the author of the image for proper permission. It is better to be safe rather than to upset anyone or violate the terms of agreement.

Dreamstime Professional Photos & Graphics

Website: http://honestholly.com/goto/dreamstime

Prior to discovering the Stock.xchng website, I have always purchased my graphics and stock photography from Dreamstime. The website has a huge variety of professional photos to use on your website or online. It doesn't matter if you are looking for vector images, health and exercise-related images, pictures of families, children, business-related images, different cultures – this website has it all.

Free Vector Stock Images

Website: http://honestholly.com/goto/freevector

Vector graphics differ from standard images because regular images are made up of grids of pixels. Vector graphics are created with paths, from point to point, with curves and angles. They can be blown up to a larger size and retain image quality, with clear edges and curves. I think vectors look modern, clean and pleasing to the eye. Some might use the phrase "Web 2.0" style to describe how these graphics look in comparison to a normal image.

Vector Portal (excellent free logo vectors)

Website: http://honestholly.com/goto/vectorportal

Free Designer Vector Images

Website: http://honestholly.com/goto/designervectors

Editing Vectors

For those who have the time, patience and interest in doing hands-on vector image editing, there are several software programs that can help you do so.

The file format for vector images are not the norm and cannot be opened and edited freely with just any program.

The top-of-the-line program to use is Adobe Illustrator. There are quite a few other choices, but that is the ultimate for the seriously interested and invested person.

For the average Joe Marketer, if you want to dabble into editing and manipulating vector images, you can use a free software program to do so. If you already have Open Office installed on your computer, the Open Office Draw program works with vectors. Otherwise, an excellent free software program is called Synfig. To learn more about it and download, please visit the website.

Synfig

Website: http://honestholly.com/goto/synfig

CHAPTER 3: OPEN SOURCE WEBSITE IDEAS

Planting Seeds of Knowledge

Now that you are aware of the infinite number of options and routes you have to take in regards to web design and development, let's go over some money-making ideas. Planting a seed is all it takes to set a person off in a direction, which can make or break his/her income. I am here to plant some seeds of Internet Marketing knowledge. You will be equipped with all of the tools you need to succeed in making a lucrative income online. Your idea is what will drive you to succeed. My ideas and advice here should open your eyes, your mind and get your thoughts rolling so you can generate money yourself.

☑ **Idea #1: Online Classifieds or Auction**

While browsing the Joomla extensions directory at: http://honestholly.com/goto/realty 📌 I found a number of free components to allow you to have your own online Classifieds ads system.

Here is an example of a website using AdManager (a Joomla classified ads extension): http://honestholly.com/goto/exampleads. 📌 My idea for someone is to create an online Classifieds website for a specific city, town or province that does not already have one. And, you'd be surprised – that (although most major cities have online classifieds) many still do not. Or, newspapers charge a person to create and post classified ads, so it would be beneficial to create one that is free for the public to use.

There are thousands of cities that you could do a quick search on Google to see if that particular city already has an online Classifieds website or not. Or, you can make a slant to the site and have it only sell specific types of items, such as: used cars or used children's items, for example. Personally, I have searched online for used Thomas the Tank Engine trains and sets and accessories. Toys (especially these popular trains) are incredibly costly.

I think that would be an excellent website idea – for someone to create a marketplace for buying, selling or even trading Thomas the Tank Engine Toys. My young son even watches YouTube Videos that little kids have created. The kids narrate their own "stories" and video tape themselves playing with the trains while telling the story.

Some of those videos have received hundreds of thousands of views. This means, my son is definitely not the only one interested in Thomas the Tank Engine. The potential there is huge. It is also hugely profitable for other popular toys. It really depends on your place of residence and the trends. It could be Barbie Dolls; it could be Hello Kitty, Bob the Builder, etc. It takes a little research and creativity, but the market is definitely there.

If you are wondering why I would give out such valuable information, rather than horde it to myself, I will explain. I can't do everything and have everything. Not only is it selfish, but I don't have time, and I want the readers of this book to know that there are so many possibilities. Do not back down or procrastinate because you see there is competition online.

You can always slant the topic or make it more appealing in some way. Take advantage of the technological advances and societal trends. You could even create a kids social network for those who love a particular toy. I know for a fact that if one existed for Thomas the Tank Engine fanatics, my son would be on there participating.

☑ Idea #2: For Sale by Owner Listings

Another website idea is to create a website which allows home owners to post their For Sale by Owner (FSBOs) home details, photos and contact info on it. This type of website could be easy to optimize if you target a specific city. If you create it about For Sale by Owner listings for a specific city, then when people go to Google to search for that, your website should ideally be at top ranking.

This would require research on your part to try to find a less-competitive city, but is certainly feasible if you follow the SEO steps in the book. The Joomla extension for this is downloadable at: http://honestholly.com/goto/mosets ✈ (this one is not open source; the cost is $119 USD). There is also an Open Realty integration for Joomla at: (free open source Open-Reality extension) download http://honestholly.com/goto/cmsrealty. ✈

☑ Idea #3: Sell Real Estate Websites

Create a real estate listings website. Without even doing any real work (just uploading the extension and Joomla files) your website will look stunning. Joomla-based sites are graphically appealing, modern and extremely attractive. Why not create a business specializing in selling real estate websites to Realtors? When I first began making money online (and my web design skills were poor) I was designing websites in Microsoft FrontPage and selling them on eBay.

In this day and age, nearly everyone has a website (for either personal or business reasons). When I first started working online, I saw an eBay auction which showed a person selling a simple Mortgage & Loan officer website (which was created in Microsoft FrontPage, and was not that fancy or appealing) and the bids were high.

It sold at $5,000.00 USD. I was shocked and dollar signs started flashing before my eyes! I must admit, I did not know about search engine optimization when I first began. That website was optimized and receiving quality traffic, and that is why it sold for so much money. But, I decided to duplicate that seller's success by creating my own mortgage and loan officer websites, full of content and ready to be used. Since I was creating the site in Microsoft FrontPage with basic HTML, I could not allow the buyer to have access to an admin panel to update or add to the site (this created future work for me because whenever they wanted updates I had to do it myself).

Now, I prefer to create websites based on Content Management Systems. That way, once the website is created for the client, I hand it over to him and he can manage it himself through an easy-to-use admin area. Some web designers would prefer not to hand-over the website, rather charge the client on a per-month basis (for maintenance and minor updates).

Long-term profits will increase and your income will become residual. It is a smart way to go if you want to solely focus on this venture (which could be very profitable). For me, personally, I started out using those methods but slowly converted into using only CMS websites, and handing the whole thing over to the buyer or client. I didn't have the time to do further updates and wanted the client to have the capabilities to do so.

If you do decide to go the route of charging a client per-month, you can setup subscription charge payments through PayPal and/or Clickbank. That way, once setup, you do not need to worry about contacting people for their payments, as the payment will automatically be withdrawn every month. The Joomla-based sites allow you to hand it over to the buyer (with the admin panel and login details so their tech or admin person can add to it whenever necessary). It saves the company a load of money that they would have spent on website updates, hiring a designer to make changes and allows the Realtor the ability to add his/her listings as he/she pleases.

You could sell these Realtor websites on eBay (be advised that you must do your research to see if you have a lot of competition on there or not – or just give it a try anyway) or you could contact real estate agents directly to offer them this service. Do your research to find the right keywords and key phrases and optimize your website to reach your target market (realtors and those in the industry).

☑ Idea #4: Business Directory Websites

You could create a Business Directory website (similar to a yellow pages or business pages) for a particular city, town or province. Once again, with Joomla there is a free extension http://honestholly.com/goto/realty ✒ and a demo website here: http://honestholly.com/goto/joomladir. ✒ The website looks professional and you can place Google Adsense ads into the pages to profit that way. You could also accept payments for the listings if you choose to because PayPal integration is already setup for you.

☑ Idea #5: Social Network Niche

Creating a social network based on a niche you are targeting is a great way to bring people together, as well as profit. People turn to the Internet for social interactions sometimes more than anywhere else. So, when someone is struggling with a problem, ailment, either mental or physical – people often go to the Internet for support and guidance.

Fortunately for Internet Marketers, there are new diseases and ailments "invented" everyday. I mean no offense to anyone by that statement, because it is unfortunate for those struggling. But, if you notice when you are watching TV, you will see new ads for medical conditions every day. If someone is looking for information and support on a particular ailment, he will most likely look online.

You could create a Social Network for a niche group of people. As far as ailments and diseases are concerned, there are so many support groups that could be created. Two quick examples of such are: adult ADHD support group or an endometriosis support group. A social network niche does not need to be related to problems – it could be related to a topic that people are passionate about. For example, I created http://honestholly.com/goto/learncontortion ✈ to group together aspiring contortionists.

I installed the Dolphin Software, which was mentioned in Book 9, Chapter 2. There already were a couple group sites for aspiring contortionists and acrobats, but I wanted one which was more professional and interactive. I'm giving it time to become fully established before charging any type of payment for services. I could allow certain members to have certain access privileges, and others to have basic privileges which would be free. It's a good way to make a residual income and help others interact.

CHAPTER 4: MASTER RESALE RIGHTS

Early on in my Internet marketing ventures and experiments online, I became aware of Master Resale Rights (MRR). The products are ones which you definitely want to have in your IM Toolkit if you want to double or triple your earnings (with no work involved in the creation process).

After discovering how to use the MRR products which I purchased, I then honestly increased my income by $36,000 USD per year.

As soon as I stopped using the technique, that income stream I created dropped off and disappeared. I had several problems with a software program I purchased (to assist me with selling these products) and to alleviate the problems I took the webpages offline temporarily. That is how I discovered exactly how much my income had increased from that one small tactic and how easily it could be obtained (and also disappear). Now that I have your attention, I will explain to people who are not aware, what MRR products are (and how you can make money from them).

Master Resale Rights (MRR)

Master Resale Right's products are licensed to allow you to resell the product (at your set price point) and keep 100% of the profits. It doesn't matter who wrote the e-book or who created the software program – if you have MRR you can sell it as if it were your own and keep all of the earnings. When you sell a MRR product, it entitles the buyer of the product to Resale Rights. Resale Rights differs because that person will be allowed to sell it, but he cannot sell the rights to his buyer. I realize it may sound confusing, but it is not overly complicated.

 Just make sure you read the terms of usage for whichever MRR or Resale Rights product that you purchase. Some of the product creators, who offer their products with MRR, require that you sell the product at a minimum price, of their choosing. Some product creators allow you to give their products away, as others do not. That's why the terms of usage should state the details and clear up any doubts or questions. If you have a website already, and are following the SEO steps to get it optimized for specific keywords, this could be an excellent opportunity for you to increase your earnings.

First, it doesn't matter what your website topic or theme is about. There are MRR products online that cover every topic imaginable.

Private Label Rights (PLR)

Private Label Rights (PLR) are also profitable, because the products licensed as PLR allow you to edit and use as you please. Editing allows you to alter content (to avoid duplicate content penalties and to provide you and your readers with unique information). For this example, let's take you through the ins and outs of MRR products and how you can profit from them.

Precautions

MRR products offered online are created by a wide range of people. Please take extreme caution before buying and before reselling the products to anyone else. Sometimes people offer such large assortments of products, that you hardly have time to evaluate the products thoroughly. In the end, the people you sell to might be upset that the information is less than high-quality. The whole situation could be avoided (and the cycle stopped) if the sellers would truly evaluate the product before reselling. I have done this in the past, like many others. When I began working online, I was focused more on myself rather than others. I learned early on that it's not about me at all, but about everyone collaborating and helping each other.

Purchasing MRR Products

MRR products can be purchased on a per-product basis or in a large grouping or package of products. I've purchased quite a few products over the years and have accumulated a large library of MRR, Resale Rights and PLR products. I've decided to offer them for sale on my website, at the lowest prices possible. So, if you want to choose from any of my products, please visit my website. I will only sell products which I vouch for 100%, so you know that what you are getting is of high quality and content.

MRR Discount Bookstore
Website: http://honestholly.com/goto/buzztopic

Profiting from MRR Products

Option 1: Selling Individual Products

There are several ways to profit from MRR products. First, if you have a website that is receiving traffic, you can sell the products on your website.

As I mentioned earlier, there are MRR products that cover every topic imaginable. So, finding one that fits in with the theme of your website will not be too difficult. If it is, you could always pay a writer to create a product for you (or write one yourself if you have the knowledge and drive) and sell it.

Option 2: Time-Sensitive Offer

This method is by far the most income-altering and profitable method to use. It is explained in depth in Book 6: Chapter 3. It was the exact method which I used when I was starting out online, and it drastically increased my income in a very short period of time. Here is a breakdown of the process:

Fill the page with either one product, several, or with a package bundled full of products related to your website (all of which are resale rights products).

Underneath your time-sensitive offer, create a link that says "No Thank You, Please Just Take Me to Download My Free Report." This way, the person has an escape route to go download the product that you were giving him for free. Some people become annoyed by these offer pages, because some webmasters make the sales pages too long and the person can't find the link to exit the page (and retrieve the free report).

- If the person clicks the "No thank you," link or decides to pass on your time-sensitive offer, then you have two options left. First, you can have the "No thank you," link hyperlinked to the actual download page for the free report (that is the nice thing to do, considering the person wanted it in the first place). The second option is one which many successful Internet Marketers employ – the Downsell.
    - ▶ The Downsell page will be a page created specifically for people who clicked the "No thank you," link and passed on the time-sensitive offer. On this page, you will offer a slightly smaller version of the original time-sensitive offer – at half of the price of the first offer.
    - ▶ Make this page short and sweet and to the point. Also, have a link on the bottom of the page that allows the person to say "No thank you," once again so he can download the free offer that he originally wanted to receive.

This technique can drastically increase your income if you have a website that is already receiving traffic. If you ever feel unsure about the process, take a look at websites of popular Internet Marketers who offer free reports. Most likely you will be taken through the exact process just mentioned. You will see how it works. Use tact and offer items of value and you'll see that backend sales can truly change your income.

BOOK 10

Holly Mann's Personal Resources

In this book, I want to share with you even more resources that I prefer to use to increase productivity and profits online.

I've tried and tested out varying techniques and software programs and continually do so. Buying software and information is very costly. It is also very timely to download, install and test out a new software program.

I've had to do everything that I can at a fast rate of speed, to save time yet measure progress. The whole purpose of the entire book is to help you create a substantial income online; several income streams that are continual in their upward growth.

I do not want you to need to test out everything under the sun, buy every product imaginable – when there might be a direct route to the solution.

People have different learning methods and approaches, but if you are struggling, my personal resources might rescue you from wasting another $30 dollars or $60 dollars on another program.

Lastly, I just wanted to state that some of the programs, software or books I will mention are free. Some of the items I mention are not free. I just wanted to reassure you that I am not shamelessly promoting these things to make a quick dollar.

I will only mention and a program if I 100% fully stand by it. If the particular program has an affiliate program with it then I may use the affiliate link in place of the normal link. I am doing this because this is affiliate marketing, and it would be a little silly to not use it (especially if I am already an affiliate).

I truly hope the resources will assist you in your day-to-day Internet Marketing endeavors.

Desktop Organization

I have created a customized image for the desktop on my computer. It is ideal for Internet Marketers, students or anyone who just wants to keep their projects, images and other folders separated nicely. You just need to download it (whichever size that would best fit your screen's resolution – I have created several different ones) & then set it as your desktop image. Then move your folders or files to appropriate places.

Formats

The images are downloadable in.png format & .psd format (For those who want to edit the file you would need to download the .psd file.)

Instructions

Download at: http://honestholly.com/goto/desktopdownload. 📌 After downloading the image you want to have on your desktop, and then find the image on your computer, view it and then Right click, hit: Set as Desktop Background.

If the image looks odd for any reason (or the wrong size) then you would possibly need to download the other size of the image and test it out. When I have time I will create more file sizes, colors and features. Right now I have created several 800 by 600 pixel resolution images, and also 1024 by 1280 pixels resolution.

Please note: I have created several different styles and graphics – some more general for anyone to use (not specific to Internet Marketers or those who are working with Honest Riches).

E-Mail Service

Gmail

I prefer to use Gmail for all of my e-mail needs. I do have several e-mail addresses though, and many of them are part of my website name. For example, help@honestholly.com could be one of them. I do not like to login to my web hosting account for my honestholly.com account each time I want to check my e-mail for that account. Instead of doing that, I setup Gmail to retrieve my external e-mails as well.

☑ **Retrieving External E-mail Accounts**

Login to the Gmail account, then click on "Settings." Within your settings, you should see a tab that says "Accounts," then scroll down until you see, "Get Mail from Other Accounts."

Get mail from other accounts:
(Download mail using POP3)

This enables you to have your external e-mail accounts, for example: help@domainname.com to be retrieved and placed in your Gmail inbox for you. It's a big time-saver for me personally. In order to setup the external account properly, you will need a few details about your e-mail account and/or hosting account. If you are using a control panel (Cpanel is common, and it is used with Bluehost accounts) – you can find the correct settings by logging into your Cpanel.

☑ **Information You Will Need**

After you click on the option to add an external account to your Gmail account, you will need to gather a few details about your web hosting.

For example, my domain name is http://www.honestholly.com and if I want to Gmail to retrieve all of my e-mails for help@honestholly.com, then I will need to provide Gmail with the specific settings related to that e-mail address (which I can obtain through the Cpanel of that site).

Login to the Cpanel, then click on "Mail."

Next, click on the link, "Add/Remove/Manage Accounts" and the next page that loads will show you all accounts you have created with your domain name. If you have not yet created one with your domain, feel free to do so now.

Configuring Mail Client for help@honestholly.com

Please select an application:

Auto-Configure Microsoft Outlook® for IMAP Access
Auto-Configure Microsoft Outlook® for POP3 Access
Auto-Configure Microsoft Outlook Express® for IMAP Access
Auto-Configure Microsoft Outlook Express® for POP3 Access
Auto-Configure Mac Mail.app® for IMAP Access

Manual Settings
Mail Server Username: help+honestholly.com
Incoming Mail Server: mail.honestholly.com
Outgoing Mail Server: mail.honestholly.com **(server requires authentication)**
Supported Incoming Mail Protocols: POP3, POP3S (SSL/TLS), IMAP, IMAPS (SSL/TLS)
Supported Outgoing Mail Protocols: SMTP, SMTPS (SSL/TLS)

Just click on the link, "Add Account," to create an account. If you are trying to obtain the proper settings (for Gmail to retrieve that external e-mail account) then look for the particular account that you want retrieved. Next to it you will see a list of options, such as: Login, Webmail, Quota, Password and Configure Outlook. Click on "Configure Outlook," next to the e-mail account you want the settings for.

Although you are not configuring your e-mail account for outlook, this page provides you with all the details that you need to forward your mail to another application. So, Gmail will require that you provide a valid Mail Server Username and Incoming or Outgoing Mail Server. All of the information you need can be obtained from this page.

☑ **Purpose**

The purpose of having Gmail pull all of my external e-mail accounts into the main Gmail account is just to save me time and keep things as organized as possible. Once the mail is in my Gmail account, I then put it under different labels to keep it even more organized.

Web Browser & Extensions

Firefox For Web Browsing

Website: http://honestholly.com/goto/firefox

I use Firefox for my web browser, rather than Internet Explorer or an alternative option. It is free, and the best thing that programmers ever created in my opinion. Switching to Firefox has been the best business and personal decision I've ever made. It's dramatically affected all aspects of my computer usage and productivity. It's safe, secure, fast, easy-to-use, with a ton of add-ons to increase flexibility even more.

Free Firefox Add-Ons

Website: http://honestholly.com/goto/addons

FireShot Add-On

Website: http://honestholly.com/goto/fireshot

FireShot is a Firefox extension that creates screenshots of web pages. I use it to take screenshots of my websites; for online tutorials and to monitor earnings. Most of the images throughout this book were taken with the FireShot add-on.

When you are on a page that you want a screenshot taken of, just click on the little fireshot box – and you will hear a snapshot (like of a camera). Instantly you will see that you have taken an image of your screen. From there you can edit or save it. You an add arrows, text or boxes or other notations to the image.

Web Developer Add-On

Website: http://honestholly.com/goto/webdevfirefox

The ultimate tool for webmasters, for those who want to edit or learn CSS (cascading style sheets) or anything else related to html or website design. After you install this add-on, you will see that you have a new toolbar in your Firefox screen. As of 2008, more than 7 million people have downloaded this popular add-on. I personally, found it more useful than all of the commercial web design and css editing programs. There are many uses for it, but I prefer to use it for CSS editing.

Purpose & Usage

It's become a difficult to task to learn how to edit different design aspects of my websites, because of my lack of expertise with CSS. For someone who does not know what CSS is, I will briefly clarify.

When a designer creates a template for a website or the actual design, he normally creates what is called a style sheet. The style sheet could be named anything, but is generally: style.css. The file type is CSS.

Style sheets must be written a certain way, or else they will not work or be valid. If valid, a style sheet will hold all of the information for all of the design elements on your website.

That way, when you want to change one thing on your site (for example, the heading font, size and color), then you would edit that in your style sheet. With one simple change to style.css, you entire design will be altered. It is a major way to save time and keep everything in one place. For a beginner, CSS can be very confusing. This Firefox tool makes it so much easier for you to learn and change your design.

Before I continue, if you need more information, guidance or tutorials about CSS, you can get them here: http://honestholly.com/goto/w3schools ✒

☑ How to Use the Web Developer Tool:

Let's say that I want to change the font size and color on my website at http://www.honestholly.com. First, I will go to the website, and then I will view my web developer toolbar.

On the toolbar, you will see: Disable, CSS, Forms, Images, Information, etc. And it continues with links and drop down menus.

Scroll over CSS, then click on "Edit CSS." You will then see that a box will appear on the bottom part of the screen. Any style sheets that are used for that particular web page will show up there (with all their coding in plain view).

For my example, I will find my style.css and I will look for the place that will allow me to view the h1 styles. I know that the h1 style is the one which makes up my homepage headings. I find the part of the style.css file which contains that information.

The h1 header code that I can change to alter the size, font or color of the headings, is here:

```
#homepage h1 {
color: #2B2B2B;
font-size: 22px;
font-family: Tahoma, Verdana;
font-weight: normal;
font-variant: small-caps;
margin: 0px 0px 5px 0px;
padding: 0px 0px 0px 0px;
}
```

So, with the split screen still open, I make the changes to the style.css. I change the font-size to make it larger (32px) & I change the font type from Tahoma to Arial. The wonderful thing about this tool is that as you make changes on the editing screen, you will see the actual alterations take place, in real time. So if I change the font size (in the editing screen) – I can then look at the page text and view how that alteration will affect the entire page.

If I want to change it more, or make it look better, I can keep making changes and viewing the results in the same screen. Once satisfied, I then save the style.css file (or copy the entire code) and overwrite that on my actual website.

So, that means, I must login to my website CPanel or file management area and find the style.css file to overwrite it with the new one. When you work with the web developer tools, you can see the changes of the page that you are editing, but it won't be permanent unless you take that code and overwrite the original file.

This tool is also neat because if you see another website online, and really like the style of their website, you can view all the code, html, php and style sheets that made it look that way. Essentially, it reveals to you how they did it – so you can replicate that if you like.

Passwords & Productivity

Roboform is one of the best productivity tools I have ever used. It is a time-saver for Internet Marketers because it keeps track of all of your login details for all of the websites you visit. It is also safe and secure. There is a free version available for download and I used that until I was ready to purchase.

Roboform

Website: http://honestholly.com/goto/roboformfree

You can download it for free. The thing I like most is the portable automated password manager, RoboForm2Go. This is also free to use, and it allows you to save all of your secure passwords on a USB flash drive.

So, you can carry all of your work with you, if you decide to work outside of your home, on a friend's computer or anywhere else. When I have had internet connection problems in the past, this was a lifesaver for me. I just took my USB flash drive (which is connected to my keychain) and plug it in at an Internet Cafe computer to do my work.

All my passwords & bookmarked sites were saved. It automatically logged me into the sites, and the information is totally encrypted and secure. None of the passwords or any information is left on the computer which I worked on.

Just pull the USB flash drive out, and take the secure password manager with me.

Web Design Software

Basic Web Design - Coffee Cup HTML Editor

Website: http://honestholly.com/goto/coffeecuphtml 📌

For basic web design and editing of html files, I prefer to use CoffeeCup HTML Editor. I think the program is simple to use, loads quickly and I like that I can use the WYSIWYG editor. It also is built-in with a lot of nice templates and layout options. It makes it extremely simple to create a website quickly.

Advanced Web Design - Adobe Dreamweaver CS3

Website: http://www.adobe.com/products/dreamweaver 📌

For advanced editing, I use Adobe Dreamweaver CS3. I prefer this when I am working with PHP files.

It is not software I would recommend for a total beginner, but for someone who is interested in advancing with web design and PHP skills.

FTP Program

My personal choice for using an FTP program is: CuteFTP. File Transfer Protocal (FTP) is a simple way to transfer files from a computer, to the Internet (or a website). CuteFTP is software that has robust features, but is simple to use. Anytime I want to update a website, upload a file or change something, I login and quickly make the changes through the interface. I've tried numerous other FTP programs but I often had connection problems or experienced extreme slowness. I have never experienced any of that with CuteFTP – so it is my software of choice.

CuteFTP

Website: http://honestholly.com/goto/cuteFTP 📌

Wink – Free Tutorial Software

Website: http://honestholly.com/goto/wink ✏

When I need to create tutorials, I generally use open source software, known as "Wink." The software makes it quite simple for anyone to create highly professional tutorials. Whenever I open up Wink and want to create a tutorial or guide, I first start by creating a "New Project." I then specify the area that I want recorded on screen.

Basically, Wink allows you to capture screenshots while you are creating a tutorial, as to walk a user through the experience. It allows you to record your voice with the screenshots if you prefer. It also allows you to create tutorial videos, by capturing a screenshot of what you are doing every time you click your mouse or move your cursor. You specify how you often you want the images to be captured.

Personally, I setup my projects to create screenshots every time I press the "Pause" key on my keyboard. That way I can manage what I am taking screenshots of, and I prefer to do still tutorials rather than video ones. Once you have enough screenshots, you can exit that mode – and edit your "slides." You can insert custom tooltips at that time, and other images and graphics to help guide the user.

Once done, you can save or output the file in one of several formats. You can save the tutorial as html (which then saves all slides as images, and that is what I prefer to do), as a PDF or as a video file.

Camtasia Studio– Tutorial Software

Website: http://honestholly.com/goto/camtasiatrial ✏

When I need to create a longer, more in-depth tutorial which includes audio and is in video format, I prefer to use Camtasia Studio. The features are robust, and the videos or tutorials which you can create with the software, are incredibly professional.

CLOSING REMARKS

Thank you for choosing Honest Riches to be your work from home, Internet Marketing guide. For more information, please visit my personal and business website at: http://honestholly.com

I provide information, free resources, web design help, productivity tips, and advice about Internet Marketing strategies discussed in this guide. I also post personal stories about life, travel, and adventures. Feel free to join in on the discussions. For those who may not know this, Honest Riches was first released in 2005. This is the final edition of Honest Riches. I plan to continue writing, learning and striving to help others.

If you are happy with the purchase and would like to earn 50% commissions on all sales of Honest Riches that are a direct result of your efforts as an affiliate, you can join my Honest Riches affiliate program.

The affiliate program signup is here: http://honestholly.com/goto/affiliates
The promotional tools, banners & ads are here: http://honestholly.com/goto/hollypromos

FURTHER READING & RESOURCES

MIKE FILSAIME
http://honestholly.com/goto/carboncopy

An expert in Internet Marketing, e-mail marketing tactics and the infamous one-time-offer pages. He is truly an Internet Marketer to keep an eye on. He has been a mentor to me from afar, and his tactics and techniques truly work. I've been fortunate to have met Mike in person, and he is a kind, down-to-earth man – skilled in what he does and helping others with the same.

JACK HUMPHREY
http://honestholly.com/goto/socialpower

Social media marketing expert and someone who totally over-delivers in his business! My dear friend Davin Ogden introduced me to the work of Jack, through Jack's Social Power Linking Website. It was the first subscription site (related to marketing) that I have ever joined and I could not be happier. His website is updated regularly and I have learned an incredible amount about social media marketing.

DAVIN OGDEN
http://honestholly.com/goto/davinogden

Viral marketing professional and truly an amazing person to know. Davin Ogden has stood by me from the beginning of my Internet Marketing career, and I have seen his life-changing influence on others. He is a light to others and has helped the masses, never asking for anything in return. He has impacted and helped me, more than he will ever know. If you are seeking more information about Viral marketing strategies, Davin is an expert.

T

U

W

www.ingramcontent.com/pod-product-compliance
Lightning Source LLC
Chambersburg PA
CBHW080403060326
40689CB00019B/4111